CASH
MACHINE

Stop Wasting Your

Organization's Money—

Start Using It to Compete And Survive

Paint, Letters and Scoop Optional

By Dan Koger, Ph.D.

Greg Brower, Ed.D.

Order this book online at www.trafford.com
or email orders@trafford.com

Most Trafford titles are also available at major online book retailers.

Printed in Victoria, BC, Canada.

ISBN: 978-1-4269-2594-8 (sc)
ISBN: 978-1-4269-2595-5 (hc)

Library of Congress Control Number: 2010901154

Our mission is to efficiently provide the world's finest, most comprehensive book publishing service, enabling every author to experience success. To find out how to publish your book, your way, and have it available worldwide, visit us online at www.trafford.com

Trafford rev. 1/29/10

www.trafford.com

North America & international
toll-free: 1 888 232 4444 (USA & Canada)
phone: 250 383 6864 ♦ fax: 812 355 4082

Table of Contents

Introduction

Goals

This book has three goals:

- Help you stop the financial bleeding at your organization.

- Help you turn your organization into a Cash Machine.

- Help you stay just ahead of the competition, forever.

But wait, you say. We're not bleeding. Sure, things get edgy sometimes. Customers push for more quality and better service. The technology tsunami keeps rolling at us. Employees want more pay and benefits. Everything keeps changing, nothing stands still.

Even so, you say, we're holding our own. As a recession raged, we kept the doors open and layoffs to a minimum. Our costs are under control and, most months, we make a profit, smaller than we might like, but profit nonetheless.

We're still alive, and we're doing okay.

And that's the problem. We'll show that when you're "doing okay," you're probably dying and don't know it. You're bleeding and can't see the blood.

You need a Cash Machine.

That's where our book can help. Continuing the hematology metaphor, we give you simple ways to find the bleeding, make it stop, help assure it won't start again, and start building the strength of your organization to survive the competitive wars.

Okay, so enough on blood. There's too much vampire literature already, without us adding to the gore. The point is that organizations battle daily to survive, a process that can get messy.

We've watched this combat from the inside, as company employees. And we've watched it from the outside, as consultants, trainers, and academics. This book is about what we learned— what works well in the survival wars, and what doesn't work so well.

Criteria

We've been tough on ourselves in writing this book. Here are the criteria we followed in preparing our recommendations for your organization. To get in our book, a Cash-Machine approach had to be:

1. **Proven**: Did we apply the approach in the past, or see it applied successfully by others?

2. **Simple**: Is the approach easy for your organization to implement?

3. **Likely to Happen**: Is there a reasonable chance the approach will be adopted, even in organizations that aren't lusting for change?

4. **Understandable**: Can we explain the approach to you, clearly and succinctly?

5. **Cheap**: Can the approach be adopted, wherever possible, by using existing resources and people?

6. **Effective**: Does the approach have a high probability of bringing you cost savings and enhanced survival prospects?

7. **Broadly Applicable**: Can the approach be effectively adopted at any organization, be it for-profit, non-profit, big, small, miniscule, religious, charitable, you name it?

8. **Short-Term or Long Term**: Can the approach be used for the quick fix of an immediate problem, while also useable as part of a continuous change process?

9. **Fun to Do**: Can the approach take some of the drudgery, and fear, out of change and more change?

10. **Fun to Write and Read**: Will this be the first business book you've read that features, among other things, the Lone Ranger, vicious tigers, phone books, front-end loaders, and piles of burning money?

There are no priorities here. Each requirement is important. After all, it's your decision whether to implement one or more of our recommendations. We want to make that decision as reliable as possible.

Kaizen

The heart of our work is a well-proven but often poorly understood organizational concept: kaizen, the Japanese term for continuous improvement.

In a kaizen organization:

- Everything that everyone does is subject to improvement at all times.

- Employees, at all levels, are rewarded for finding opportunities for improvement, rather than punished for "doing something wrong."

- Employees are trained, and retrained, to use a reliable problem-solving system to turn "problems" into improved work processes.

- Leaders, at all levels, enable employees to find and fix process problems

There are other things that go on in a kaizen organization, but that should help frame your thinking.

Kaizen is powerful stuff—so powerful that it can save, or kill, your organization. We use narrative and graphics to make this case.

Companies that have worked hard over the years to understand and apply kaizen have benefitted handsomely. As Exhibit A, we offer the Japanese car makers, with Toyota leading the pack.

Unfortunately, many organizations, including alarming numbers in America, haven't paid their kaizen dues, and now face a terrible price for their lapse. As Exhibit A of failure to pursue systematic, planned continuous improvement we offer America's car makers, once giants of the industrial world and now woefully diminished enterprises fighting to survive. As former GM employees, we had ringside seats for early stages of the disaster; a heartbreaking sight to behold.

We give reasons why some organizations embrace kaizen, and why others overlook, or overtly reject it. We discuss the benefits of kaizen, and the dreadful costs of ignoring it. And, most important, we devote most of this book to describing affordable, accessible, and, we hope, creative ways that your organization can access the many benefits of systematic continuous improvement.

Cash Machine

Simply stated, a Cash Machine is a machine that dispenses cash. Done the way we recommend in this book, kaizen can turn your organization into a Cash Machine that literally dispenses money. By that we mean kaizen can serve up found money to your organization, money that you'd otherwise be wasting on recurring problems in production, personnel, customer service, marketing and other activities.

We illustrate our Cash-Machine concept with a really big front-end loader. The idea is that you can use kaizen to literally scoop piles of money off the organizational scrap heap and redirect it to productive and profitable uses—research and development, better marketing, more employee training and re-training, and enhanced customer service come to mind.

Without kaizen, money lost to recurring problems and errors is money that is <u>lost</u> forever. With kaizen, money gained by permanently resolving production and service problems is money that is <u>saved</u> forever. When you run your organization as a kaizen Cash Machine, continuous improvement is the gift that keeps on giving.

We're here to help you build <u>your</u> financial front-end loader—your Cash Machine. How you use all that extra cash is up to you. After all, it's your Cash Machine.

ISO and Kaizen

Briefly, ISO is a set of standards that help establish best practices in multiple functions of an organization. It's a myth that the letters ISO are an acronym. They're not. Instead ISO is derived from the Greek word *isas*, meaning *same* or *equal*. ISO standards are maintained by a non-government organization in Geneva, Switzerland. <u>Any</u> organization, from a one-employee bagel shop to a huge multi-national, is a candidate for ISO certification.

We present ISO certification in this book as a way to jump-start your shift to a continuous-improvement, kaizen company. Put another way, ISO can be the early blueprint for your Cash Machine—a quick, effective and affordable way to get into the kaizen game.

ISO certification is concise, specific, tangible and relatively inexpensive—an ideal way to start building your Cash Machine. Ideas in this book help you get the most from these first ISO efforts.

Organizations receive ISO certification by passing an audit of work processes that reflect their ability to identify, remedy and, where possible, prevent <u>recurring</u> service and production problems, with the key word here being "recurring."

Awareness of ISO and continuous improvement in the American business psyche isn't the problem. Each year thousands of organizations get ISO certification, from sprawling corporate multi-nationals and behemoth government agencies to one-employee machine shops.

The problem: these recipients don't take their ISO certification far enough. They stop with certification and miss the real rewards that ISO can bring as a jump starter for continuous improvement. Said another way, they miss the chance to leverage ISO into their organization's Cash Machine.

Instead, they settle for an ISO banner above the front door to satisfy a demanding customer or keep up with a challenging competitor. After certification, little else changes, and that's the problem.

For the financial and competitive payoffs of ISO certification to flow into your firm, you must rearrange your thinking, starting with the leadership team. You and your colleagues need to see ISO certification as a <u>gateway</u> to bigger things, not as an end in itself. Your ISO investment in time and dollars starts paying off when you use your fresh new certification to set the stage for deep commitment to, and employee performance of, life-long, managed continuous improvement.

When you do that you've taken the first step to turning your organization into a Cash Machine.

We can help.

Dan and Greg

Dan Koger

Over the past 25 years, Dan has provided consulting services in organizationalcommunications, group-performancedevelopment, process improvement, change management, conflict resolution, presentation skills, customer service and quality improvement. Clients have included such giants as AT&T, General Motors, Johnson & Johnson, IBM, and Nortel, with many assignments requiring extended work in Europe, Asia and the Middle East.

He has a bachelor's degree in journalism from the University of Missouri, a masters degree in American economic history from Michigan State University, a doctorate in American Studies/ Communications from Michigan State University, and certification in Strategic Business Planning from Wharton School of Business at the University of Pennsylvania. He is currently an associate professor of communication at Lindsey Wilson College in Columbia, Kentucky.

Greg Brower

Greg Brower, an International lecturer and consultant in quality and continuous improvement, has been President of GAB Consultancy in Simi Valley, California, for the past 15 years. He worked closely with quality mega-gurus W. Edwards Deming and Philip Crosby and has been personally authorized to instruct and consult on their principles and practices.

Greg is among the few Americans who have consulted on quality and continuous improvement to Japanese industry. Massaki Imai's book, *Gemba Kaizen,* notes some of Greg's thinking.

As a founder of the General Motors Quality Institute, Greg had the unique experience of applying key quality philosophies to the test of daily application. He now helps client organizations put these capabilities into daily practice.

Greg holds a bachelor's degree from Wayne State University, a master's degree in Management from Central Michigan University, and a doctorate in Management Education from Western Michigan University. He also has a certificate in Strategic Business Planning from Wharton School of Business at the University of Pennsylvania.

You can reach Dan or Greg through:

GAB Consultancy

3420 Whispering Glen Court

Simi Valley, California 93065

(805) 522-0286

Email: gab4iso@aol.com

Our Commitment

We've read our share of business books; seldom a happy experience. Business books can be preachy, convoluted, boring and sometimes down right wrong. In this book we promise to be truthful, accurate, and interesting. We also promise not to take ourselves too seriously, not only a reasonable idea but also a fundamental edict of kaizen. People with inflated egos aren't always the best candidates for the kaizen world, where a willingness to scrap old ways and adopt new ones is a way of life.

We have a track record in this regard. Our last book was about the three-dimensional nature of workplace problems, and the need to take a three-dimensional approach to solving them. Our model for this was a Rubic's cube orbiting the earth. As noted, in this book you'll meet up with tigers, burning piles of money, front-end loaders, the Lone Ranger, and more.

Plus, in the world of writing, kaizen is known as "editing." As an ex-newspaper reporter and journalism teacher, Dan takes editing very seriously. He's hard on our writing to the point of personal pain and suffering. Every word must count, or it's gone. Every line must mesh with our selection criteria, or it's gone. Dan's editing is not a pretty sight, but it's what we think it takes to bring you a business book like nothing you're read before.

So let's get started.

NOTES

Chapter 1

Your "Cash Machine:"
Paint, Letters and Scoop Optional

Imagine this.

Your organization has never been so strapped for money. You've downsized, throwing some of your most valuable people over the side to save scarce payroll dollars. You've postponed essential research and development projects, prayerfully hoping the whole time that your competitors don't come up with a game-changing breakthrough. Banners festoon company walls urging employees to conserve everything from paper towels to ballpoint pens.

And yet, in the midst of all this scrimping an annual ritual unfolds.

Accountants total the money your company still wastes each year on such systemic rat holes as warrantee payments, product and service rework, often accompanied by angry or lost customers, inspection and more inspection of products and services, workers compensation premiums, work place injuries, resignations of top employees, and other recurring, resource-sucking activities.

Let's peg the number at $5 million, more for larger companies, less for smaller ones.

Now imagine that amount in the form of five million one-dollar bills, heaped in an ugly green pile in the middle of the employee parking lot, with employees and leaders gathered around chanting "burn, burn, burn."

Executive aides with cans of gasoline soak the money.

Then, as employees watch breathlessly, company leaders hurl matches into the fuming mass. Flames roar. The sky turns a $5-million shade of orange.

But wait! Now imagine this.

As those loyal aides finger their cans of unleaded regular someone in the crowd, armed with a really loud bull horn, shouts:

"Wait right there! Why are we doing this? That's our money! Why are we wasting it, especially during these perilous times?"

At which point a wizened veteran of dozens of these fiery rites slowly rises and says: "It's what we've always done, young man. It has to happen. We cannot stop it. It's just a cost of doing business."

The bull-horn-toting skeptic stands his ground, or her ground. The rebel raises the bull horn and blares:

"Why don't we stop piling up all that wasted money in the first place?"

To which that aged guardian of company culture snaps, with a withering air of finality: "And how would we do that?"

Seizing the moment, our trouble maker shouts into the bull horn, "bring in THE RIG."

Suddenly a gate opens and in comes a massive yellow front-end loader.

Reaching the money pile, the loader driver lowers his scoop, hauls up a hefty helping of doomed dollars and gently drops them into a bin marked "Research and Development." The driver takes another scoop of loot and drops it into a bin marked "Employee Training." The scoop keeps digging until all the dollars are in bins, bound for improved productivity and higher profits, not fiscal blood letting.

Painted in big letters on the sides of the rumbling yellow money scooper are the words "CASH MACHINE."

Where do you get such a wondrous contraption?

Simple. You build one, using resources you already own

All you need to get started are a couple of well-known, if under-used and often misunderstood war horses from the world of quality-management:

- Kaizen/continuous improvement, a technology that dates from roughly the dawn of time.

- ISO certification, a technology that dates from roughly the 1980s that can give you a jump start on becoming a kaizen organization.

But wait. Don't savvy organization leaders already know how continuous improvement and ISO certification can help save lots of dollars in the short run and very likely save their organizations in the long run?

Some do. Tragically, though, many more don't. In fact, too often leaders don't even give it a try. Reasons abound. Here are some that we hear:

- "Who needs continuous improvement? We're already the best in the business. No one can lay a glove on us."

- "Never heard of ISO certification. What in the world is that?"

- "Continuous improvement—isn't that a Japanese thing? We're Americans. We run things our way around here."

- "ISO! No thanks. That's just another pack of government regulations."

- "Continuous improvement! That's a lot of hooey. Any idiot knows if it ain't broke, don't fix it."

- "ISO certification costs an arm and a leg, and we'll have nothing but a piece of paper to show for it."

- "Continuous improvement and ISO would mean change. Forget it. Too much disruption here already, especially with the economy in tatters."

- "We already have ISO certification. Didn't you see the banner over the front door?"

- "We've been around for decades. We'll be here for a lot more, no matter what."

- "Sales have never been better. Why spend money on lots of change that we don't need?"

- "Maybe someday, but not now. There's a recession on. We can't afford it."

The list goes on. For now, let's cut through the objections and get to the real questions:

- Will you be the wizened veteran standing in the glow of your burning money who insists: "We've always done it that way; who needs the change?"

- Or will you be the bull-horn-toting skeptic who shouts: "Why?"

While pondering your choice remember what we discovered years ago— complacency can kill you.

In Chapter 4 we draw you a picture of how this happens, using what we call the "Organizational Survival Model." On the model, you can track your organization's place in the unending race to survive in a world of blinding change and innovation.

In such a world, a moment's lapse can drop you hopelessly below what we call the Change/Tech Curve—the third rail of organizational survival. You may dig out from your first trip below the curve, through heroic spending, horrific struggle and frenzied, unmanaged change.

Dip below the Change/Tech Curve a second, or worse, a third time, and your survival chances approach zero. Masaaki Imai, father of the concept of "kaizen" continuous improvement, summarizes your possible situation this way. "Without continuous improvement," Imai says, "your organization's name may no longer be in the telephone book."

Try phoning someone at Lehman Bros., Circuit City, or Oldsmobile. Sorry. No one home.

It's all about the change you want at your organization—managed or chaotic, constant or periodic, routine or frenzied.

If you want managed, constant and routine change at your organization, we can show you how continuous improvement, led by ISO certification, can help. In our approach, ISO certification is

5

your guide, your "kaizen classroom." The continuous-improvement systems that emerge from a companion "ISO classroom" drive your never-ending management of change—your Cash Machine.

Paint, letters and scoop optional.

NOTES

Chapter 2

Adopt "Kaizen" Values
And Philosophy;
Your Cash Machine Will Follow

In our opinion, the recent deep recession that impacted your organization, as it impacted most of the economic world, could have been prevented or cushioned with a lot more continuous improvement and ISO and a lot less business bravado, financial gimmickry, fads and flawed assumptions.

As the challenges continue, we offer what quality guru W. Edwards Deming called, in his bestselling book of the same name, a way "Out of the Crisis."

Hundreds of business fads have come and gone in the years since Deming, Joseph Juran, Phillip B. Crosby, Kaeoru Ishikawa,

Masaaki Imai and other total-quality gurus pioneered the concept that all employees of an organization should at all times be actively pursuing ever-improving levels of product and service quality, customer satisfaction, process performance, and waste reduction.

That's the ideal, one that eluded far too many American companies in the past, and still eludes too many of them today.

It doesn't have to be that way.

Let's take a close look at kaizen, jump started by ISO certification, as a way to get past issues and misunderstandings like those noted above.

Stamping out recurring, money-draining organizational problems is the heart and soul of continuous improvement and ISO opens the door to continuous improvement.

Kaizen brings in the cash by routinely allowing all your workers to identify and eliminate problems that have been plaguing your organization for days, weeks or even years, and at considerable recurring expense.

What are these "considerable expenses," and the recurring problems that drive them up and up?

Remember the organizational bon fire in Chapter 1? We think such a thing is hardly an exaggeration. The tragic reality is that organizations routinely pour buckets of money down myriad rat holes as they encounter, and bandage over, the same problems again and again. They even create "first aid stations," in the form of rebuild, rework, or warranty operations, devoted entirely to putting costly bandages on problems that should systematically be eliminated.

Think of continuous improvement as a set of principles and practices devoted to getting companies out of the first aid business and into the job of getting full return from their production dollars, whether in factories or offices.

Let's continue that "first aid" analogy for a moment.

Suppose your joints ache and your body temperature is 100.6 degrees, two degrees above normal. You visit a doctor, who gathers basic information about you and your illness. Some of this information may be qualitative, in the form of reports by you of such things as where it hurts, how long you've been ailing and whether you have any chronic disorders that could contribute to your fever and achiness. The doctor may also gather quantitative information, in the form of temperature checks, blood-pressure readings and laboratory analysis of blood, urine or other fluids.

Based on this information, along with his or her prior experience in treating such conditions, the doctor will formulate a treatment plan focused on the root cause of your illness, not just on your symptoms of fever and achiness. Well-trained doctors know that something is causing these symptoms and that the treatment must address the cause, not the symptoms.

Why can't such thinking be transferred to our plants and offices, where costly symptoms of underlying problems are so abundant?

Consider employee tardiness and absenteeism as a relatively simple example. Let's adopt the assumption that all employees want to do a good job, even though many managers who "just know" the people who look to them for leadership really want to find every possible way to dope off and make mistakes on the job.

Such thinking keeps disciplinarians in the human-resources department busy. But it doesn't do much to fix underlying employee problems.

We take a more positive view of the matter. Look at your own work-place behavior. Do you want to do a good job, we ask you? Of course, you reply. Do you remember when you interviewed for your current job, we ask? Of course, you reply.

How many times in that interview, we ask, did you tell the interviewer that you wanted to do 93.5 percent good work during your years with your prospective employer? Or that you wanted

9

to be on time to the job no less than 92.6 percent of the time? Never, you reply. Your commitment then, and now, is to achieve what the quality gurus call "zero defects," a concept with a crucial place in the underlying philosophy of continuous improvement.

Okay, we ask, how come you've had your share of process problems and errors over the years—being late, absent, or unprepared? Were those "defects" caused by your determination to mess up? Or were they caused by circumstances you didn't know about, or that were beyond your control, including misunderstandings, that you wish hadn't been there? Circumstances, of course, you say.

Okay, goes more of our argument, if the problems in your career were caused by circumstances external to you, what some might call "the system," what should you attempt to fix, the person or the system?

Thinking driven by the spirit of continuous improvement would focus on finding out what's wrong with the system, and improving it so those defects never happen again. The workers, including you, are an innocent bystander in such a scenario. You're also the person, along with your colleagues, who should be trained and empowered to devise and implement those improvements.

If you're a leader, you focus on the systems and work processes in your organization. You train all your employees to work on the systems and processes, because these are the things that define each day of their working lives.

In other words, like that doctor we discussed above, you and your people find and fix the root causes of system problems. That's continuous improvement.

Simple enough, we hope you're saying to yourself about now. But don't most rational people in the world of organizations already find and treat the root causes of problems, especially recurring problems, instead of reprimanding the employees who, in the minds of leaders, "caused this mess?"

Don't you believe it. In our experience, treating symptoms, not problems, is the norm. In fact, in many cases organization leaders institutionalize the treating of symptoms, and do it, oddly enough, with considerable pride of accomplishment.

Consider a visit we made a few years ago to a plant making engines for a prestigious and once dominant brand of luxury American automobile.

The plant manager proudly walked a group of visitors through the assembly area, where we watched dedicated employees carefully inserting pistons into engine blocks and torquing down cylinder-head bolts.

Then he took us to what he said was his favorite place in the production area, the place where the best and the brightest of his workforce, the people with the most creativity and skill, toiled day and night. And what were they doing, these crème de la crème employees? What they were doing was applying "band aids" to a never-ending series of pricey symptoms—in this case in the form of repairing engines that didn't pass final inspection.

These defective engines were the very expensive "culls" from a very expensive production system. Over and over and over, day after day, month after month, these top employees labored, secure in the knowledge that the flow of engines into rework was steady and predictable.

"Aren't they terrific," the plant manager bragged as he gazed admiringly at those busy engine re-workers, their arms elbow deep in the bowels of brand new, yet already ailing auto power plants.

That car company, by the way, recently filed for bankruptcy and is now trying to find a place for itself in a global car and truck industry that it ruled with an iron fist not so many years ago.

Did that plant manager have the power to assign his best and brightest employees to finding the root causes of those failed engines, and fixing the systems that created such failures?

Sure he did, but he didn't make the assignment. He wasn't committed to the concepts and techniques of kaizen.

And that's where much of the problem lies in today's plants and offices. The skills of continuous improvement aren't all that obscure or challenging. We provide quite a few of them in this book. Anyone can learn to do problem solving that's focused on fixing root cause, not symptoms. We even give you a simple process for finding and fixing root cause, a process you can start using and teaching tomorrow—if you choose. And the choice is always up to you.

Band aid or permanent corrective action? You decide.

We preach that it's not the skills among managers and senior leaders of organizations that's the problem. Those can be taught. It's the attitudes, perspective and values of kaizen that are lacking. To do kaizen effectively, everyone in an organization, from the top down, has to think in terms of constant, relentless pursuit of improvements, no matter how small. With these views in place you can become a "kaizen" Cash Machine company, with this book as your guide.

The rest of the Cash Machine process is primarily technique, something you can be taught, in this book, in myriad training programs, and with ISO certification as your jump start into the kaizen game.

In a kaizen company, employees are rewarded and celebrated for finding problems and leading systematic efforts to fix them, forever. Leaders bring awareness to all employees that a few small but vital ways of doing things differently, of taking control of work processes, is an essential, life-saving, and highly valued task.

What a refreshing difference that is from a work world of blame, recrimination, anger and revenge.

The choice is yours.

Chapter 3

Kaizen and ISO;
Gold Mines That
Can Save "Your Company"

What are the financial stakes of making that first ISO-driven leap, with kaizen to follow? For more on that question, let's take a closer look at our auto-industry plant manager and the dollars he was wasting with his much-admired repair and restoration group.

Here's some simple addition and multiplication. Suppose his elite engine plant "Emergency Room" employed about 20 of the organization's most skilled workers.

Let's say that each of those skilled savers of busted engines earned $40 per hour in combined pay and benefits. That's $320 per day, per worker, hardly a monster sum at a corporate giant with many tens of billions of dollars in annual sales.

But wait. There are 20 of those engine magicians in the rework department. That means the company spends $6,400 per day just on rework payroll, a heftier sum but still miniscule in the great order of things for such a grand organization.

So let's continue our math trip. That per-day payroll, times five days a week, is $32,000, every working week, presumably forever. Multiply that by four weeks a month and our rework payroll has ballooned to $128,000 per month.

Multiply that by 12 months of the year and you have a rework payroll of $1,536,000—a tidy sum by our humble standards for a single plant. How much research and development could you fund for $1.5 million? How many additional workers could you hire? How many shareholder dividends could you send out?

Multiply that $1.5 million by a hundred plants. That gives you an annual company-wide rework bill that tops out in the $150 million range.

Welcome to that bonfire out in the employee parking lot. You can generate quite an impressive glow in the sky with that amount of money.

Of course our calculations are crude, to say the least. There are many more hidden costs of funding rework—floor space, tool costs, lighting, you name it—that we didn't tabulate. But the costs are there and they keep rolling along

But wait, there's more. How about the cost of inspecting those engines in the first place? Some of the best people in plants and offices are assigned to be inspectors, often at top salaries.

Even so, inspectors aren't super human. Some make mistakes. So what about the engines the inspectors miss despite their best efforts, the ones that end up in cars that customers buy and then bring back to their dealers for warranty repairs?

How about, for the sake of simplicity, we tack on an extra $2 million per year to our single-plant rework bill for such incidentals as physical space, inspection and warranty. That gives us a total of $3.5 million per year for "rework," again at only one plant.

Multiply that by 100 and the glow of burning money out in the parking lot becomes really impressive. A Cash Machine that could spit out a found $350 million, year after year, might be kind of handy.

And what about that annual cost-accrual issue? The simple fact is that your organization is wasting that money year after year. The cost of rework, like rust, never sleeps.

Get into a serious battle with technology creep and aggressive cost cutting from competitors and those rework "bandages" can kill your organization.

An ISO-continuous improvement Cash Machine is what you build in your plants and offices to stop hemorrhaging cash from those "recurring" problems.

In our view, you will stop the bleeding and start building your Cash Machine when two things happen:

1. Leaders ask: "why in the world are we paying our best employees to redo the work that we just paid other employees to do the first time?"

2. And then leaders say: "give us a system that stops this madness, now!"

Continuous improvement is that system, and the way to jump start that system is ISO certification.

Now let's take a closer look at continuous improvement.

A discussion of continuous improvement begins with one of those quality gurus—this one Masaaki Imai, the acknowledged father of "kaizen," the Japanese term for continuous improvement.

Imai's bestselling 1986 book, *Kaizen—The Key to Japanese Competitive Success,* establishes the foundations of what now is known as "lean manufacturing," the concept of doing more with less that we offer in this book.

Greg had the good fortune of delivering a series of performance-improvement seminars with Imai in South Africa. In that time he got a deeper look into the guru's views of what seems like a simple concept, fix things all the time, that isn't quite that simple after all.

Imai, like us, has seen gains in the use of continuous improvement by American companies over the years. But he, like us, also sees lots of opportunities for companies around the world to make far better use of kaizen.

In a 1996 interview with the journal *Quality Digest,* Imai was asked: "What impact do you think kaizen has had on U.S. companies?"

Imai reminded the interviewer, and the readers, that "kaizen" means "ongoing improvement involving everybody, without spending much money" and that "American companies have made great strides in improving product quality," and that much of that gain has been "attributable to their implementation of *kaizen* principles."

But Imai saw the need for much broader adoption of kaizen in America. In the context of the Change/Tech Curve that we introduce in Chapter 4, his words should generate a bit of management reflection, to say the least:

> *Many companies still have not fully embraced the kaizen concept, although I suspect they would argue with me about my comment. But I see a lack of kaizen when I look at how companies address the actual cost of making products. Most companies still subscribe to the old paradigm which says that better quality costs more money. The real challenge to management is to improve quality while reducing cost because that is what today's customers want.*

And there you have it. Masaaki Imai says more American companies need to adopt the principles and practice of "kaizen."

"That is what today's customers want," Imai declared in closing his interview.

We couldn't agree more.

In our view, continuous improvement/kaizen is the relentless, daily salvaging of otherwise lost money. It's that money that funds the Cash Machine.

It's your money, after all. ISO and continuous improvement—the Cash-Machine fundamentals—let you capture money you otherwise lose and put it to better use—developing new products and services, monitoring customer needs, saving jobs—the choice is yours.

Great idea? You bet!

Wish we'd thought of it.

Sure, we came up with the idea of building an organizational "Cash Machine" to describe what ISO and continuous improvement can do for you and others.

But the thinking that makes the Cash Machine possible belongs to the ages.

Consider, for example, the men and women since the dawn of the species who've tried to get the most from scarce resources. After days hunting wooly mammoths, our ancient forebears couldn't have thought well of leaving useful mammoth meat behind.

More recently, the *American Heritage* Dictionary tells us that the proverbial saying "waste not, want not," dates from a 1576 assertion that *"willful waste makes woeful want."*

We couldn't agree more. "Willful waste" indeed.

Moving on. In the 18th century, that guru of all things wise and useful, Benjamin Franklin, reminded us humans that "a penny saved is a penny earned." In that same vein, Ben said there's "a place for everything, and everything in its place," and that "a small leak can sink a great ship," words of wisdom recent GM leaders might take to heart.

It was the frugal Japanese who refined the wisdom of Ben Franklin and those wooly mammoth hunters into a competition-beating business philosophy—one that puts leaders and workers in a relentless hunt for waste, not once in a while, but every hour of every day, forever.

A modern-day Ben Franklin in the war on organizational waste was Taiichi Ohno, a legendary productivity expert. In the 1940s Ohno set Toyota on the road to what would become known as the "Toyota Production System," a lean manufacturing method that has helped make life miserable for America's Big Three Automakers, among others.

Critical to Ohno's system of waste-busting, and to the building of your organization's Cash Machine, is awareness of what Toyota and other quality-conscious organizations around the world call "The Seven Wastes." Cash-Machine companies put everyone to work, all the time, seeking to eliminate:

1. Defects in products or services

2. Over-production, with accompanying high set-up and storage costs

3. Waiting for materials or services to arrive

4. Transporting, the time and money spent in carrying products or services within a location, or from one location to another

5. Movement, the time wasted as workers are forced to move in acquiring resources needed to do their jobs

6. Inappropriate processing, added steps that don't add value within a work process

7. Inventory, the cost of marshalling and storing materials that aren't immediately used and that hide defective parts

We're not here to teach you the advanced nuances of Toyota Production or The Seven Wastes, as tempting as that might be. Perhaps another book for another day.

What we want is to outline a few relatively simple steps American business leaders can take to do what lean manufacturing companies have been doing, on an organized basis, for decades—saving money and other resources by systematically using them more wisely.

Can Americans wage war on waste, or has our cultural devotion to planned obsolescence and throw-away resources so marred our thinking that we can't shake the habit?

Sure we can. If Ben Franklin could do it so can today's American business leaders. All that's needed is the right insight and a lot of practice.

ISO certification is where your war on costly waste begins—the first step in creating your Cash Machine. Combine your ISO certification with the kinds of total quality and continuous-improvement basics we provide in this book and you're on your way to saving costly resources and perhaps beating the competition in today's fight for survival.

Put another way, you're on your way to assuring that your organization keeps its name in the telephone book.

NOTES

Chapter 4

Keeping "Your Company" Alive

"Kill the company!" That's a little strong, you say.

Believe it, and here's a picture of how it happens, what we call the Organizational Survival Model. The trajectory of your company in the world of change is labeled, appropriately, "Your Company." We'll get to the line labeled "Kaizen/ISO Company" shortly; building and sustaining a Kaizen/ISO Company is what this book is about.

The Organizational Survival Model

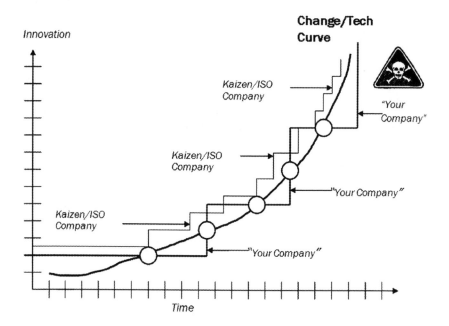

See that Change/Tech Curve looping gently upward through the center of the model? As we said earlier, think of that as the "third rail" that's waiting to kill "Your Company" if you touch it or worse yet, slide below it.

The vertical axis of our model is Units of Innovation; the horizontal axis is Time. The Change/Tech Curve tracks the accelerating nature of innovation over time, especially today, as digital and related technology turns business assumptions upside down on a daily basis.

If the human brain was hard-wired to keep up with the Change/Tech Curve we might not be having this discussion. But that's not the case. Instead, even with all the innovation and creativity the mind can produce; our brains are still prone to building paradigms—a framework of assumptions and beliefs about the way the world "really is."

What this means for "Your Company" is simple: leaders, and employees are grasping the implications of yesterday's or today's business "reality" just as the lethal Change/Tech Curve is hauling that reality to tomorrow's newer, and inevitably higher level. The temptation is for "Your Company" to rest, perhaps just for a moment, comfortable in the assumption that the firm's products, services, customer base and "competitive edge" are safely ahead of the curve.

That's where the trouble begins.

Humans rest; the Change/Tech Curve never sleeps. It never assumes things are okay for now, or that innovation is slowing down. Just the opposite. On the Change/Tech Curve, innovation speeds up.

The fearsome reality at "Your Company" is this: someone, somewhere in the world is busy inventing new techniques and technologies that will erase the competitive edge you think you have. And how's this for scary. In most cases you don't even know it's happening—until it's too late, or, if you're lucky, almost too late.

Here's a tale of two nightmares showing the Change/Tech Curve in action, one involving victims and the other involving a company that moved the Change/Tech Curve to a new plateau. America's car makers stand out as curve victims. These once-mighty "Big Three" firms made products that flew out the showroom door in the decades after World War II, until one day they didn't.

Suddenly these proud giants were fighting for their lives in a world filled with global products that customers liked better than theirs. Or how about the American television, clothing or even bicycle industries? Same story—gone or on life support.

And then there's the story of Apple computers and the now famous iPhone.

In the 1980s Apple fell from industry dominance to virtually second-class citizenship. The founder and former CEO Steve

Jobs retook the reins of his old firm and started innovating with a vengeance. There were pastel computers, bigger screens on laptops, increased computing speed, simplified operating systems and other improvements.

Then, in mid 2007 came the iPhone and suddenly every other firm in the cellular phone business was fighting for its life. Jobs had put an entire industry below the Change/Tech Curve. In today's world of change, the game can be turned inside out in moments. You may not be the Apple of change in your line of work, but by practicing daily kaizen/ISO you can be ready to adapt quickly, because everyone, and we mean everyone, in your organization is already used to living in a change-rich environment.

Companies without such adaptation skills have a much harder time digging out from under a tsunami of change. They touch the third rail of the Change/Tech Curve, then let themselves get behind it. When you're behind the Change/Tech Curve the rational world disappears. Heroics are daily events. The call goes out to the "Lone Ranger," the jaunty risk-taker, the merciless "turn-around" artist, to save the day, white horse and all.

Frenzied restructuring, mass lay offs, government bailouts, devastating and often ill-advised mergers—you name it—are the norm as these would-be "heroes" struggle to revive the dying patient. What should have been a never-ending series of small, well-managed adjustments and improvements over time has now become major surgery.

Pick your industry—computers, telecommunication, entertainment, finance, agriculture, even charitable giving. They're all being wracked by relentless change. Companies struggle to keep up. Some succeed, which in the context of the Organizational Survival Model only means that they live to change and innovate the next day, and the next one after that, forever. Hewlett-Packard, Apple, and AT&T are some of the firms that have recently survived such massive change efforts.

Some, including Oldsmobile, Lehman Bros., Knight-Ridder newspapers, didn't make it. As Masaaki Imai, the kaizen guru, said at that training session Dan attended, you can't call these organizations on the telephone because "they're no longer in the phone book."

Heroic leaps from below the Change/Tech Curve into new levels of competitiveness are, to say the least, risky. Steve Tobak, writing in the on-line business web site BNET in mid 2009 commented on the findings of the consulting firm McKensey & Company that two-thirds of major change management efforts will, and should, fail.

He argues that when leaders have to "save the company" there's no guarantee that they'll do the right thing. Adrift in uncharted waters, they're likely to <u>guess</u> about what to do, to grasp at what "seems right." Under such urgent conditions, risk assessment may be diminished or discarded entirely.

Tobak offers an example:

> *The CEO gets it in his head to take the company somewhere, the board bites, and off it goes, risk analysis be damned. I can think of a dozen other failure modes, but it's mostly about the inherent risk in strategic change. If your strategy is right half the time, you're doing pretty well. But what about the other half of the time?*
>
> *If I'm not mistaken, executives develop the vision, strategy, goals, plans - all that good stuff - and then start the change management process. Sometimes the CEO does it in a vacuum.*

Mergers, for example, are a favorite strategy in trying times, again with no guarantee of success. As examples of flawed mergers, Tobak offers the recent experiences of such respected corporate giants as **Sprint-Nextel** and **AOL-Time Warner.**

Recent flawed "turnarounds" include **Gateway, Nortel, Jerry Yang's Yahoo and Carly Fiorina's** restructuring plan for **HP**.

"They failed," Tobak writes, "not because of flawed process or methodology—but because they were bad ideas to begin with and the employees probably knew it."

Part of the reason they were "bad ideas," we maintain, is that they were made in an atmosphere of crisis and desperation, the kind of thing that old western hero, the Lone Ranger, used to thrive on.

In a Lone Ranger adventure, "someone has to do something" was the mantra chanted by frightened townspeople, cries for help taken by the Lone Ranger as his cue to ride to the rescue. In modern times, in the real business world, chief executives imbued with hefty doses of the Lone-Ranger ethic take over the situation with six-guns blasting. The company's fate is on the line, after all. Dramatic action must be taken.

How could board members say no, or even ask hard questions, under such conditions?

That's one of the major risks when companies have to claw their way from below the Change/Tech Curve. There's no time. The Visigoths are at the gate. Frantic measures are hurled into the breach in lieu of well-planned, manageable units of change executed from a position of strength as a continuing way of corporate life.

Desperate times do often call for desperate measures, which is one of many reasons to avoid desperation wherever possible

Here's how we've seen the "desperation scenario" unfold again and again.

Assume "Your Company" isn't using kaizen/ISO as a way of organizational life, especially in such key areas as customer relations, human relations, training, communication, and leadership commitment.

Yet, absent the principles and practices of continuous improvement, "Your Company" still manages to sail through seven years of innovation leadership, with everyone enjoying the prosperity this brings.

And then one day "Your Company" hits the Change/Tech Curve. Sparks don't fly, bells don't ring, sirens don't wail. It's just another day at the office, with one notable exception. In the competitive world out there, "Your Company" is now just another player in your industry, with no measurable technological advantage, no competitive edge. Your lead is gone, and you and your colleagues probably don't even know it.

Now comes the lethal part of the Organizational Survival Model. That's when "Your Company" sinks below the Change/Tech Curve, all the time blithely doing the very things that made you successful for the previous seven years.

Given another year or so of the kind of prosperity that comes from doing things the way you always did them, and you're in big trouble.

Now you're pleading for your corporate Lone Ranger to ride in and jump-start that old and much-loved prosperity that has somehow "slipped away." You're scratching for money to fund frenzied research and development. Employees are "downsized," a particularly objectionable euphemism for "fired and it's not their fault."

But wait! Let's assume that the Lone Ranger arrives just in time, as is often his unique gift. Frantic change is thrust upon all members of "Your Company", and by some miracle you survive the ordeal. The Masked Man has saved the day once more at yet another beleaguered organization, always at considerable gain to his bank account and considerable cost to employees, shareholders and other stakeholders. Loyal and skilled employees of "Your Company," the ones who brought success in the first place, are long gone. But, halleluiah, "Your Company" is again slightly ahead of the competition, and miracle of miracles, by approximately the same distance that you enjoyed eight or nine years earlier.

Only this time, because the Change/Tech Curve is always getting steeper, you have significantly less time to enjoy your dominant position.

For the survivors, the Apples and Hewletts and AT&T and such that live through a climb from below the Change/Tech Curve to a restored position of leadership, life hasn't gotten all that pleasant.

That's because "Your Company" and the others must struggle even harder to avoid bumping into that third rail again, this time with far less margin for complacency or miscalculation because the pace of change has accelerated and the time for recovery is shorter.

Fail a second time in your duel with third-rail levels of market and industry change and the journey upward will be far longer, harder and scarier, and with significantly lower potential for survival despite your most valiant efforts.

Try these heroics a third time and "Your Company" probably won't live to tell the tale. You'll go bankrupt, be swallowed by a competitor, or muddle along as a bit player in a fast moving industry. No matter what happens, it's "game over" for "Your Company".

We'd like to make a simple suggestion, backed up by decades of experience with kaizen/ISO. Fire the Lone Ranger, or better yet, don't hire him, or her, in the first place.

In reality, being the Lone Ranger is fine so long as you have a large supply of "silver bullets," and abundant chances to use them. Sooner or later, though, even the Lone Ranger is going to run low on ammo, and opportunity. Plus, don't forget, the guy wears a mask, even on hot days, sleeps under the stars even though he can afford a decent hotel room, never gets dirty, and has no visible means of support.

Here's a different possibility. Instead of relying on risky heroics, simply structure and sustain "Your Company" to continuously ride the powerful waves of change that you know are coming at you, forever. Operate so that the forces of change don't bury you from time to time, until one day you just can't manage that one last dramatic recovery and "Your Company's" name drops from the phone book.

Instead of drama and heroism, use kaizen/ISO an integrated system to manage change in bite-sized pieces, every hour of every day, in most cases using existing resources.

Become the Kaizen/ISO Company on the Organizational Survival Model, the one that stays just ahead of the lethal Change/Tech Curve, always.

How far ahead? Not very. You don't have to stay far ahead to survive. Here's a fable from Maasaki Imai, our kaizen guru, which makes our point about minimalism winning the survival wars.

Two men were hiking in the jungle one day when they came to a wide clearing. As they started walking across the clearing a huge tiger leaped from the trees and started chasing them. The men ran as fast as they could go, but, little by little, the tiger kept gaining on them. Suddenly one of the men sat down on a rock, whipped off his backpack, and pulled out a pair of running shoes.

"Are you insane!" said his companion. "Why are you wasting time changing your shoes at a time like this?"

"So I can run faster," said the first man.

"But those shoes won't help you run faster than the tiger," said the incredulous observer.

"I don't have to run faster than the tiger," said the first man. "I only have to run one step faster than you."

That's the reality of continuous improvement. You only have to stay one step ahead of the Change/Tech Curve, and the competition, but you have to do it every day, with many small improvements across the organization. These changes in turn drive a clear survival strategy that never assumes invincibility and never rests on today's market leadership.

In the coming chapters we'll share ways we've used over the years to help organizations get just ahead of the Change/Tech Curve, quickly and economically, and with the least amount of change-based disruption to the work force, and then stay there.

If you're an organization leader you have a clear choice regarding the Change/Tech Curve. "Your Company" can rely on the frenzied management techniques of the Lone Ranger, an 80-year-old mythological cowboy hero with silver bullets, a fast horse and interpersonal-skills issues that make him wear a mask all day.

Or you can rely on "Your Company" as a Cash Machine that always keeps just ahead of the Change/Tech Curve, and just ahead of the competition. With kaizen/ISO you can harness the power of kaizen/continuous improvement, a timeless business technology that focuses the collective wisdom of all your employees on the systematic quest for small but significant improvements in all your work processes, all of the time.

The choice is yours.

NOTES

Chapter 5

Myths and Realities
Of a World-Changing
Technology

What happens to the Cash Machine, we often ask? Why do perfectly rational business leaders turn their backs on the found money and enhanced prospects for survival that we just illustrated?

We have a theory. We think it's often about the myths that have grown up around kaizen and ISO over the years, myths that too few people take the time to challenge.

A first step in seizing the kaizen/ISO potential is to know something about why firms fail to seize such opportunities in the first place. If you see your organization enmeshed in one or more of these myths, we hope you'll consider rearranging your thinking.

Let's start with one of the most destructive myths to dog kaizen/ISO over the years:

<u>Myth</u>: ISO certification somehow solves your quality, productivity and customer-service problems in a single burst of activity.

<u>Wrong</u>: We want to drive a stake, once and for all, through the heart of the belief that ISO certification means your problems are over.

By itself, what ISO certification means is just what it says—you're ISO certified. Too often this consists of hanging an ISO banner above your front door, having a celebration with cake and punch, and then going back to doing things the same way you always did, without exploring the possibilities of the technology you just paid for.

The profound truth about ISO is that payback for your certification efforts is all about what you do after you've stepped through the ISO certification door.

We try to present ISO certification to our clients as a first step in the endless pursuit of continuous improvement—a pursuit that requires relentless attention to such things as training, strategic planning, constant and enlightened communication with stakeholders inside and outside the company, focus on constantly understanding customer needs.

Too often, organizations break kaizen and ISO apart, with ISO certification being handled as a limited and tangible event that meets momentary customer requirements or passing competitive demands of the market place. Subsequent pursuit of quality and continuous improvement, if they're considered at all, are often filed under "work for another day" as the ISO banner is nailed up.

The harsh truth is this. In today's fearsome business world ISO has to be far more than a banner over a door, or a few words down in the lower left-hand corner of company business cards.

We want you to see ISO as the blueprint for "Your Company's" Cash Machine.

We'll return to the mechanics of ISO as a blueprint for progress in later chapters. For now, let's move on to a few of the other kaizen and ISO myths—what they are and what they aren't, starting with a definition of the term "myth."

We consider a myth to be "an unproved or false collective belief," with the operative word being "collective." Kaizen and ISO have certainly collected their share of "unproved or false beliefs" over the decades, and lots of people who believe them.

For example:

Myth: ISO is an acronym standing for something like "International Standards Organization," and that ISO is a branch of one or more governments.

Wrong: ISO is a set of standards that help establish best practices in multiple functions of an organization.

Contrary to what many believe, ISO is not an acronym. Rather, it is a derivative of the Greek word *isas*, meaning same or equal.

Organizations receive ISO certification by passing an audit of work processes that reflect their ability to identify, remedy and, where possible, prevent recurring production problems.

ISO standards and auditing practices are maintained by the International Organization for Standardization, an independent, non-government agency headquartered in Geneva, Switzerland.

ISO describes itself, in its official web site, as a "**network** of the national standards institutes of **161 countries**, one member per country, with a Central Secretariat in Geneva that coordinates the system."

ISO, according to the site, is a "bridge between the public and private sectors. On the one hand, many of its member institutes are part of the governmental structure of their countries, or are mandated by their government. On the other hand, other members have their roots uniquely in the private sector, having been set up by national partnerships of industry associations."

Due to perceptions of higher quality products and services, companies with ISO certification often have an edge over competitors, so long as they use sound continuous-improvement practices to sustain that edge.

Myth: If we ignore the need for ISO certification and continuous quality improvement maybe our problems will just go away by themselves.

Wrong: Change, especially in organizations, can't be stopped, as we saw earlier. Your change choices are limited. You can create company systems that guide the power of change for your corporate gain. Or you can ignore the need for small, incremental, continuous change and risk facing a dramatic, expensive and potentially fatal tsunami of change later.

Our thinking is simple: ISO Certification is an important first step in developing the processes and behaviors that position "Your Company" to handle change, and the challenges that come with it. With Continuous improvement in work processes and customer service, you can adapt to change in small doses, managed by design rather than by fear and luck.

Ignoring change, or hoping it will go away, can set up your organization for overwhelming change down the road, with accompanying pain and cost.

Myth: We're in the middle of a recession; there's no way we can justify spending time and money on ISO certification and the implementation of kaizen business practices.

Wrong: Thomas Friedman, Pulitzer-Prize-winning author of the best-selling *The World is Flat* and many other books and articles on change in today's global economy, recently offered a positive view of business opportunities in today's recessionary economy, but only for organizations equipped for deep and rapid change and adaptation.

"Historically," Friedman wrote in the New York Times, "recessions have been a time when new companies, like Microsoft, get born, and good companies separate themselves from their competition. It makes sense."

So how do organizations become Friedman's "good companies," thriving in the midst of major economic challenge?

"When times are tight," Friedman writes, "people look for new, less expensive ways to do old things. Necessity breeds invention. We...can only invent our way back to prosperity. We need everyone at every level to get smarter." (Emphasis added.)

And how can organizations make sure that "everyone at every level" is getting smarter? What we've been saying since page 1—obtain ISO certification as entree into the world of continuous improvement, with accompanying systems that effectively track process performance and stimulate creative process improvement.

Can American organizations cope with economic adversity? Friedman thinks so, if they choose the route of adaptation and continuous improvement. "I still believe that America, with its unrivaled freedoms, venture capital industry, research universities and openness...has the best assets to be taking advantage of this moment — to out-innovate our competition."

But for Friedman and others, there's no time to waste. "We should be pressing these advantages to the max right now," he says.

Myth: ISO certified companies produce quality products; once we're certified our problems are over

Wrong: ISO Certification provides tools and concepts that can help guide organization leaders and workers in the continuing quest for improved processes and increased customer satisfaction.

In a free-market economy, an ISO-certified company can, for example, produce and attempt to sell lead life jackets. Unfortunately, no matter how well made, these products won't satisfy a basic requirement of life jackets—that they need to float. ISO-required systems for gathering customer data would likely soon show that customers were less than pleased with such a product.

ISO-mandated tracking systems will generate the valuable data you need to understand your work processes and your customers' needs. But decision makers will have to act on this information— or continue to sell market-negative products. ISO certification is like any other business tool—nice to look at, but useless unless used effectively by well-informed, perceptive and skilled leaders and workers.

Myth: ISO certification is only for the big guys.

Wrong: Size definitely doesn't matter in the world of ISO. We've gotten ISO certification for one-man operations. You don't need big budgets and lots of people to enter the world of ISO and continuous improvement.

What you need is commitment to cutting production costs by documenting key elements of your production processes, including recurring root-cause analysis of problems that are sapping your dollars and manpower. Then you need systems to identify ways to improve those processes so the problems go away, forever.

You can satisfy the workforce training requirements of ISO by teaching your employees simple steps to find and permanently eliminate these costly challenges.

Myth: ISO certification means our company will have to do more inspecting.

Wrong: ISO certification can, and should, be your ticket to less inspecting, not more. In the ISO world, inspection is considered a "Price of Non-Conformance." In other words, using inspectors to discard goods and services before they're sent to customers is a kind of surtax you pay for defective production processes—a tax you pay indefinitely, unless you take what is referred to in ISO as "Permanent Corrective Action."

The costs of inspecting can be prodigious. Let's look at a few:

- Salaries and benefits for inspectors

- Cost of physical support for inspectors, including office space, tools, and other resources

- Cost of materials and time to craft products and services that are ultimately discarded

- Potential negative impact on customer satisfaction if defective products or services get past the inspectors

- Potential legal liabilities if defective products or services get past the inspectors

- Potential negative impact on the morale of workers

- Diversion of scarce time, money and creativity that could be otherwise devoted to innovation, and the improvement of processes and customer service

Myth: ISO certification is only for manufacturing companies.

Wrong: If your organization provides products or services to customers, you're definitely a candidate for ISO certification. All organizations have work processes, so all organizations have opportunities for process improvement. ISO Certification gives you a chance to "jump start" the kinds of activities and behaviors that lead to better, more cost-effective, ways to do what your organization already does.

Myth: ISO certification creates a paperwork nightmare.

Wrong: ISO requires that you maintain specific, and limited, documentation of process performance and the things done to improve that performance. In most cases, ISO companies end up eliminating paperwork that doesn't directly contribute to Quality and Productivity. We'll take a much closer look at ISO and the value of documents in the next chapter.

Myth: ISO certification is just an "add-on" to impress customers and suppliers

Wrong: You can use ISO Certification as an add-on, an array of extra activity that has no discernible impact on change and performance. That's the very thing we're attempting to address in this book. Done properly, ISO and continuous improvement become part of the way you do business, not something you point to when customers come to visit.

Myth: ISO and kaizen/continuous improvement are just fads; these too shall pass

Wrong: You can treat kaizen/ISO as if they were fads, the latest miracle process or technology that will solve your production problems and save "Your Company". That too will fly in the face of what we're trying to say in this book. ISO and continuous improvement have been staples of high-performing companies around the world since before World War II. Their capacity to improve performance in small increments, day after day, was proven long ago.

If anything, kaizen/ISO has been around long enough to have lost its flashy sheen. It's not billed as the latest "quick fix." Instead it represents a way of life that you and others can pursue, or ignore, as you see fit.

Myth: ISO certification is expensive and time-consuming to obtain, and requires lots of expensive new equipment and operating systems. After our investment in time and money, ISO certification will be a net loss.

Wrong: The basic requirements of ISO certification can be rapidly attained and highly affordable. The question is what your organization does with the insights and opportunities ISO offers.

The best and most economical way to begin your ISO experience is with a commitment to use existing systems wherever possible, but with an enlightened new quality-improvement twist. In other words, even with ISO certification, you don't need to buy it if you already own it.   For example, with the techniques of ISO, you can use fresh insights and techniques to examine your levels of production waste, including waste of time and materials.

Instead of writing these off as merely recurring costs of doing business, you can start recording these numbers, and then viewing the resulting data as guides for opportunities to improve. Doing this will demonstrate that you are practicing kaizen. Also, by measuring evidence of waste in production you will have taken the first step in establishing your "Permanent Corrective Action" system.

Both of these are ISO requirements. Your ability to adapt existing company resources is limited only by your creativity and your commitment to process improvement.

Congratulations!

With ISO certification you're on your way to getting better performance from what you already own.

As human constructs, companies and even entire markets behave pretty much the same way: You lose your job and can't afford a new cell phone or a better phone plan, so Verizon buys less from its vendors, everybody in that food chain cuts jobs, and that brings us back to the beginning. It's like a giant flywheel that feeds on itself.

Except in a serious financial crisis, like the one we're in now, it's the same effect in pretty much every market: automotive, food, clothing, energy, electronics, housing, telecom, you name it. As a result, every individual, family, and company is on alert and braced for impact. And that even includes the relatively healthy ones.

The cynical among you might say CEOs are protecting their bonuses. That may be true, but the bonus targets are usually derived with some degree of corporate health and shareholder wealth in mind. Like it or not, that's the way the system works.

Anyway, sooner or later we start to see indications that a few of the flywheels are slowing down, indicating the beginning of a recovery, although each flywheel recovers at a different rate. For example, a recovery in consumer staples may precede a recovery in luxury items.

Eventually, though, it's good times again.

NOTES

Chapter 6

Kaizen/ISO—The Foundation Of Your Cash Machine

As we've said, with Kaizen, jump started with ISO certification, your organization has a chance of keeping its name in the telephone book, or in today's digital world, on the internet.

So now you've made the decision to go for ISO certification. What are some of the concepts, principles and requirements you will encounter.

Here are a few:

Controlling Processes and Eliminating Waste

Kaizen and ISO are all about finding countless ways of doing work more efficiently, and with continuously decreasing amounts of waste.

Consider documentation and paperwork as an example.

As any business person knows, you manage your paperwork, or it manages you. The myth is that ISO creates more paperwork. In fact, ISO helps you reduce paperwork; you keep the documents you need for continuous improvement, as determined by your ISO certification audit, and dial back on everything else.

It's all part of that same simple truth of ISO and continuous improvement—when you're running a Cash Machine the focus is always on eliminating waste, not creating it. This includes the waste of time spent on unproductive paperwork that doesn't make a proven contribution to continuous improvement and customer satisfaction.

In an ISO Company employees search for ways to simplify documents. They systematically discard superseded documents, and eliminate documents and forms that aren't making measureable contributions to productivity.

Here's Masaaki Imai's view of the matter in his *Quality Digest* interview:

> Everybody in the company *should be seeking a better way of doing their job all the time by constantly eliminating muda (nonvalue-adding activities) and streamlining the work processes, and managers should be establishing a challenging target to motivate employees. (Emphasis added)*

Unproductive documentation, whether in paper or digital form, is definitely "muda," a polite Japanese term for junk that can be tossed over the side.

In this mindset, documentation that makes the ISO cut allows everyone at your organization to track improvements that have been made, and identify opportunities for more improvements.

The principles behind ISO documentation are simple and powerful—make all those motivational words and commitments visible. Show visibly, for example, that employees are being trained in effective problem-solving systems and that they are using these systems regularly and well.

Show that you hear the customer's voice by reflecting these needs on charts and grafts that everyone can see and study. Show that customer words and admonitions are being translated in your organization into the language of marketing, engineering, research and development and other disciplines.

ISO says "show" visible evidence that this information is being converted into better products and services for these same customers.

ISO also asks that organizations visibly identify the key processes upon which they depend for survival and show that these processes are constantly being improved. Simple process mapping will satisfy this requirement.

Leaders of ISO organizations are always aware of money, but not necessarily as an end in itself. ISO companies operate on the principle that income and profits reflect customer satisfaction and continuous improvement. Profits come when costs go down and productivity and sales go up. No mystery there. Money is one of the ways to *visibly* track these business indicators. In the Cash Machine, money is a measure, not an end.

Money isn't the reason for the ISO organization to exist—tracking it is, as a means to learn more about how processes are working, as we show in more detail in Chapter 11.

In summary here, when organizations see themselves as existing primarily to make money, to keep those 10-day sales figures up, to jack up those executive stock options, some very specific employee values and behaviors emerge, ones that, recent economic events reveal, don't always bode well for customers, stockholders, executives, employees, or tragically, the public at large.

When, on the other hand, the organization sees itself as existing to continuously improve customer service while eliminating waste in all parts of the operation, including documentation, very different values and behaviors emerge—ones driven by substance instead of financial voodoo.

Reduced to its simplest terms, we counsel clients that ISO Standards require only that you maintain a Quality Manual and practice a handful of quality procedures. Don't over-document your systems, creating needless processes and work instructions. Over-documenting can bring three major problems:

1. Extra dollars and time spent create documents that don't do enough work for you

2. Creation of reams of paper that nobody reads (except the auditor, if that)

3. "Handcuffs" that lead your organization into needless rigidity, potentially impairing flexibility in reacting swiftly to changing conditions, including new customer mandates.

Let's make it even simpler. For ISO certification, you only have to meet three documentation requirements. You need:

- Visible statements of your quality policy and quality objectives,

- A Quality Manual,

- Documented process procedures for six important activities in the organization: document control, control of records, control of non-conforming product, internal audit, corrective action and preventive action.

Your ISO consultant should provide templates for each of these requirements. If they don't, get a new consultant.

The Quality Management System:
How to Operate Your Cash Machine

Let's revisit that employee parking lot for a moment, the one where $5 million worth of dollar bills is stacked in a gasoline-soaked pile.

Who throws the match that turns all that wasted money into a pile of useless ash?

Not employees. They stand there and watch, most of them mesmerized by the ritual of it all, some resigned to the reality that "that's how we do things around here," and a few angry that their jobs are trifled with so senselessly, and frustrated by their powerlessness.

Not stock holders. They aren't even invited to the party and can only judge that something is amiss when organization performance figures deteriorate, as they inevitably do.

Not customers. Most don't know such dramatic waste is happening, until, perhaps, they demand higher quality at lower prices from the organization, and consistently see that their needs aren't met.

No, it's management that orders that wasted money to be stacked in the employee parking lot. It's management that calls in those loyal underlings with their cans of unleaded regular. And finally, it's management that tosses lighted matches into the money pile, creating that dramatic blaze.

If you're a manager, in other words, it's your money pile. You mandated its creation and it's you who lit the fire. The whole annual smoldering mess belongs to you. The defining concept of this principle is that nothing happens in an organization unless management wants it to happen. Managers aren't paid to build cars, diagnose customer technology needs, or drive trucks.

Managers direct others to do these things. Managers determine if employees are doing the right things, with the right resources, at acceptable cost. If customers are happy and the organization prospers we can assume that the managers are doing the right things.

But managers can also mandate employee behaviors that disappoint customers in one or more of the three basics of enterprise—cost, quality and delivery. When this happens, problems ensue.

In the fundamental logic of ISO and continuous improvement, these are management problems, not employee problems. Let these situations continue—miss customer targets too often and for too long and the Change/Tech Curve starts creeping above your horizon. We've already discussed what that can mean—pain, rising costs, dropping revenues and ultimately questions about the survival of the organization.

The ISO certification process can be your ticket to new thinking about the meaning of managing and leadership of others.

We could write an entire book about ISO, continuous improvement and the role of managers. We'll keep our views here to a few paragraphs on the subject; you can decide where you want to go after that.

When ISO auditors visit, they want to see evidence that managing is a full-time occupation at your organization—that members of the management team get out of their offices, visit the workers where they do their jobs, get involved in identifying and solving problems, and generally behave as if continuous improvement were a real organization priority.

The auditors don't want to see motivational posters in the work areas, or flashy banners festooned with the latest company slogan. You can put them up if you want to, but the ISO auditors won't be impressed. They want to see the visible footprints of continuous improvement, not talk, smoke and mirrors.

Here's a few of the things auditors do to prove that management has the necessary skill and insight to build and operate their Cash Machine.

First, they want to see your *Quality Manual*, the book that spells out how you constantly mobilize everyone, and we mean everyone, in the organization to seek improvements that better meet customer expectations.

We spent time on the myths of ISO and continuous improvement a couple of chapters ago. Here's where one of the ISO myths gets exploded. The auditors don't particularly care how you word your commitment to continuous improvement and customer satisfaction in your *Quality Manual*. They just want you to show them written, visible evidence that you have methods in place for achieving these goals and that you are deploying, reviewing and revising these commitments and techniques throughout the work force, and that you do this every day.

Next, the auditors want to see your written *Quality Policy*, a well-phrased statement that establishes how you pursue continuous improvement and why. They'll talk with workers to establish how well this policy is known and understood on the plant and office floors.

Included in the *Quality Policy* will be reference to hearing the voice of the customer, and how you turn that voice into constant changes that advance customer satisfaction.

Here's where many of our ISO clients take this part of the certification process to highly advanced levels. They practice what the Japanese call *hoshin kanri planning*, where detailed company-wide objectives are turned into specific behaviors by each employee in each part of the organization. In Japanese, *hoshin* means shining metal and compass. *Kanri* means management or control.

The name suggests how *hoshin* planning aligns an organization toward accomplishing specific goals. Articles on the subject often include a picture of a compass.

ISO and the Resources for Your Cash Machine

You can't run your Cash-Machine organization without basic resources, such as buildings, office space, machinery and access to people who can support your efforts. ISO takes this into consideration.

You can be a one-person operation and hire or borrow many of these resources—using a spare bedroom as a home office, with Kinko's for copying, faxing and mailing, and so on.

Or your organization might be a multi-national behemoth with whole divisions of support staff.

Managing all this comes down to the same Cash-Machine principles of customer focus and process control that we've been talking about since the Introduction

ISO has only a few words on this, all of them related to giving employees what they need to do a good job. According to the ISO standards, managers and supervisors need to provide employees with physical resources, prioritization of assignments, training, implementation of the Quality Management System, a system for continuous process improvement and the means to enhance customer satisfaction by knowing and meeting customer requirements.

As always, the ISO regulations require minimal documentation for all this, including records of education, training, skills development and on-the-job training. Under the best possible conditions, you'll need to develop multi-disciplinary teams to get maximum performance in pursuit of continuing customer satisfaction.

Here's a final word on all this. ISO wants you to figure out what your organization's objective are. Then it wants visible evidence that you're communicating these objectives to members of the work force. Hoshin kanri happens when you successfully mobilize workers to fully understand their roles in making these goals happen.

With ISO, in other words, all you have to do is focus the organization on the customer, establish goals that lead you to fulfilling customer needs, train and focus workers, and encourage everyone to continuously improve everything they do.

That sounds easy enough. But then, we ask, if it's so easy why doesn't everyone do it?

There are several more ISO focus areas that will be part of your ISO audit—processes in purchasing, product design, customer communications, and production being a few of them. There aren't many, but they are the process areas that make a critical impact on your organization's prosperity and survival.

We could go into more detail on these and other ISO categories, but that's another book.

Suppose, instead of jumping into ISO certification right away, you just want to try a few kaizen activities tomorrow? The next few chapters contain things to think about, and to do, to start making the transition to a kaizen organization with a more assured place in the telephone book and on the internet.

We start with basic kaizen-based problem solving.

NOTES

Chapter 7

The 3-D
Problem Solving Process

In any kaizen organization, you need a way for <u>all</u> employees to continuously identify, analyze and solve problems wherever and whenever they occur. As noted earlier, the trick here is to quickly identify the root causes of problems, so employees don't waste valuable time struggling with symptoms.

We offer a 3-D approach to problem solving in the work place, since most problems occur on multiple levels that you have to dig through to find out what's really going on—without getting bogged down in "paralysis by analysis."

2-Dimensional problem solving can make you crazy.

In this chapter, we show you why this happens, and then give you a way out of the asylum—using a proven process that focuses the collective wisdom of problem-solving groups on a straight-forward objective—fixing what's wrong.

We'll have some fun along the way, while pursuing a serious goal—helping you and your colleagues diagnose the root causes of work place problems, and eliminate them forever. Students of total quality will recognize this as "permanent corrective action," the Holy Grail of quality improvement and a worthy objective for anyone trying to do good work and beat the competition.

The Rubic's Cube is our symbol for the 3-D nature of real-world problems. The world is a 3-Dimensional place, after all, with height, width and depth, just like a Rubic's Cube. Real-world problems are 3-Dimensional too, with multiple layers of interconnected causes demanding multiple, interconnected solutions.

When we attribute colors to categories of problem causes, as we do later in the chapter, you'll see that any problem quickly becomes multi-dimensional and multi-colored—again a Rubic's Cube, if you please.

Until you learn how to solve a Rubic's Cube, one of these little chunks of interconnected plastic can drive you nuts. A multi-dimensional problem, with interconnected layers of cause and effect, can make you just as loopy, until you learn how to manage these kinds of challenges with equal dispatch. Our goal is to give you just that capability.

We focus on problem solving in organizations, but our 3-D Problem Solving Process can be applied anywhere things go wrong—schools, families, communities, nations, you name it. All you need to get into the 3-Dimensional problem-solving business are two or more well-intended people, a few sheets of flip chart paper, some felt-tip markers, a couple of packages of sticky notes—and our process.

What we offer here is a problem-solving system that quickly allows you and your colleagues to see and manage the depth and complexity of multiple causes, with solid, effective, real-world solutions to those causes.

Put another way, we're committed to helping you take the blinders off so you can see and manage the complex world of problem solving in all its polychromatic and multi-dimensional fullness.

As these pages unfold, we have two basic objectives for you.

First, we want you to understand the fundamental pitfalls of traditional, 2-Dimensional problem solving, why it falls short in today's complex organizations and how it can make you nuts. Then we want you to see the benefits and applicability of our 3-Dimensional approach to fixing what's wrong.

We're practical guys, from the trenches of organizational America, so we know that understanding something isn't enough. You have to put that understanding to work or the value is lost. Our 3-Dimensional problem-solving approach has to withstand the relentless pressures of daily business operations. If you can't put it to work on *the job*, solving problems and saving money, than it's worthless.

We'll take you, step by step, through this approach. By the time you finish this chapter, we want you fully equipped to fix real, 3-Dimensional problems in your organization, as a matter of routine.

We'll show you how to work quickly with others, breaking problems down to their multiple root causes. Then we'll show you how to harness the collective brainpower of your work group or team in finding and applying solutions to each of these causes.

Finally, we'll show you how to put your solutions into an implementation plan with a high probability of:

A. Being executed by the right people in the right places and,

B. Bringing measurable gains to your organization

Successful implementation is huge in the practical world where we do our consulting, and we want it to be just as huge in yours. That's why we'll also show you how to "bullet-proof" your implementation plans in ways that lower the prospect of derailment down the road.

While we're on the subject of "bullet-proofing," here's a word of caution. We know it's a demanding environment out there, and you, like most, are probably in constant pursuit of shortcuts— ways to get from Point A to Point B faster than the next guy. Such motivation is commendable. But in the context of this book, it could also have undesired consequences.

Our caution is this. You may already suspect that something is wrong with the way things currently get fixed in organizations and that a 3-D approach like ours is just the ticket. As a result, you may be tempted to skip the first part of this book and go straight to the problem-solving system.

We urge you not to.

We guarantee that many others in your organization aren't as insightful as you are. You'll need colleagues in your camp if you're going to get the most from of our system, as we point out in the section on teams and work groups.

This chapter will give you the concepts and words you'll need to convert a few "Lone Rangers," "Attila the Huns," or "veterans of the last war" to your 3-D view of problem solving.

"So, how do I know that this 3-D system works?" you might legitimately ask.

To address this, we offer a brief look at our track record over the years in developing what has now become 3-D Problem Solving. Here are a few examples of the many ways this approach has given organizations documented competitive advantage.

A cross-functional team at a major multi-national pharmaceutical company was responsible for managing regulatory issues for a drug product worth more than $2 billion in annual sales. After a year together, the team was losing its focus. At the end of an eight-hour problem solving and strategic planning session, our 3-D approach allowed the team to identify its few vital issues and clarify its primary objectives.

The core elements of what would become a detailed action plan were identified at that same meeting. This was the start of an 18-month engagement that saw the product through numerous marketing and regulatory challenges around the world. The team ultimately saved the firm hundreds of million of dollars annually in potential lost sales, and won the company's highest team-performance award.

A major high-technology firm wasn't meeting the complex needs of banks, phone companies, retail giants and other customers. Sales and repeat business were at risk or already lost. Cross-functional teams were developed to apply intense focus on the unique needs and concerns of individual customers. Each team was trained to use an early version of what later evolved into 3-D Problem Solving. They could now quickly identify the root causes of customer problems, and establish in-depth solutions for them.

Ultimately, more than 400 such teams were established at the company's many locations around the world, with accompanying gains in sales totals and service satisfaction.

A nation-wide corporate relocation company with headquarters in Orange County, California, had established itself over many years as a quality leader in its industry. A glass case in the headquarters lobby was filled with trophies and certificates recognizing ISO quality certification, customer satisfaction achievements and continuous improvement leadership.

What the company didn't have was 3-D Problem Solving to get a grip on persistent organizational and customer challenges. During a one-day session in the spring of 2003, leaders of the company identified $500,000 in potential operational and service gains, using 3-D Problem Solving techniques. At the end of the day, group members had identified root causes of some of the company's most persistent problems, prioritized which solutions to apply in which order, and developed a detailed implementation plan to assure that the solutions were realized on schedule.

First, our 3-D approach is best done in small groups, where group members can bounce ideas off each other in a controlled environment during any number of brainstorming sessions.

This doesn't mean you can't use the 3-D process without others to help you. When working alone, you can still get the advantage of <u>visually</u> examining the process. The important thing is that you put your best ideas on a flip chart directly in front of your eyes, where the words are nice and big and the imprint on your brain, through your eyes, is also nice and big. You'll also need to transfer your flip-chart ideas to sticky notes so you can examine different combinations of causes and solutions, as we explain later.

When working alone, you're best off doing everything we outline on the following pages, flip charts, sticky notes and all. Trust the process and it will work for you.

For our purposes here, assume you and your associates are working together as a small group, say four or five members. Remember, it doesn't take a big crowd or a permanent team to use this process. All you need is a handful of people, sharply focused on a problem and equipped with a problem-solving process that can help you get to the hidden causes that are costing your organization time, money and other scarce resources.

Here's how you can start working with our 3-D approach to permanently solve work-place problems.

These are the basic steps we'll take you through to attack a tough problem. We'll examine each step in detail and show you how to use each one as effectively as possible:

- *Step One:* Define the Problem

- *Step Two:* Identify Causes

- *Step Three:* Sort Things Out

- *Step Four:* Prioritize

- *Step Five:* Find the Root Cause

- *Step Six:* Create Solutions

- *Step Seven:* Check and Repeat

- *Step Eight:* Create an Action Plan

- *Step Nine:* Document Gains

- *Step Ten:* Teach Others the "3-D Approach"

Please note the order of these steps. It's important. This is a systematic process, so you'll need to follow the steps each time in the order provided. That's because there are some obvious dependencies that need to be respected. Jump out of order and you risk sliding back into the world of 2-D problem solving, where quick-fix artists eyeball a situation, reach a snap conclusion, impose a "common sense" solution and walk away, leaving you and your colleagues to deal with whatever unintended consequences that might arise.

We're out of that game now. We trust our process, a powerful strength of which is its sequencing. Let's take a moment to reinforce that strength with an example from our consulting work. This will illustrate the importance of dependencies, while also giving you a good preliminary look at the mechanics of the 3-D problem-solving process, including the interaction of flip charts, sticky notes and brainstorming.

We often find ourselves helping groups with the basics of process mapping. Working with the group, we use various symbols, such as squares, diamonds and ovals, to create a visual "process map" of the various steps required for a work system to function.

The advantage of process mapping is that it allows everyone involved in a process to actually see, sometimes for the first time, what they do, where they do it in the process, and also, importantly, how what they do is dependent on the work of others, and how others are dependent on what they contribute.

That's where the real world of interconnectedness starts to come to life for people in the work place, as in a revelation such as: "I always assumed that you put five foot-pounds of torque on that degauser nut and now you tell me you actually only put three foot-pounds of torque on it. That changes everything."

We return now to our list of steps in the 3-D Problem-Solving Process, but with the admonition that you and your problem-solving colleagues do not, repeat, do not pass up Step One. Failing to clearly define the problem you're working on together is an invitation to disaster.

Failing to clearly and mutually define the problem can cause everyone a tremendous amount of confusion. How can you find causes, let alone root causes, when you don't even know, collectively, what you're trying to fix? In the same vein, how can you sort and prioritize causes if you haven't identified them yet.

And then there's one of the worst offenders—identifying a solution and starting an implementation plan before digging into potential causes and spending some time drilling down into root causes. Doing this puts you right back with the Lone Ranger and Attila the Hun, tossing out those quick fixes without learning exactly what it is you're trying to fix.

So once again, trust the process. Respect it and it will take care of you.

Step One: Define the problem

As noted earlier, it's critical that you put the problem definition in writing, preferably on a flip chart. If you're facilitating the group through the process, ask questions about the wording. Test commitment to the words you've chosen as a group.

Make sure all team members agree on the wording before continuing on to the next step. Be especially mindful of the ideas from those closest to what has gone wrong. This, like other steps in the process, may take a bit more time in the short run, but it will save time down the road. In addition, you will be winning over helpers with your efforts by enrolling them early in a process to eliminate problems that have probably been bothering them for some time.

Once you're sure everyone is satisfied with the wording of the problem definition, tape your flip chart sheet with the definition on it to a prominent spot on the wall of the room where you're meeting. There's a strong prospect that you'll refer back to this definition as you move forward in the process, especially if conflict arises over some of the causes, or which solution should be implemented in which order.

The problem definition will serve as a pillar in your conflict-management efforts. Instead of arguing over abstractions, or the ideas of one person versus the group, you have a written, visible, mutually crafted problem definition to point to as a tiebreaker. You'll be discussing visible specifics instead of mysterious abstractions.

The problem definition statement also gives you an anchor to tie down later decision-making. It will help keep everyone on track through each of the other steps.

Step Two: Identify Causes

Now that we agree on the definition of our problem, we're ready to begin surfacing its many underlying causes.

Here, again, brainstorming will be an important group-management tool. We want to surface as many reasons as possible for the problem to happen, no matter how far-fetched some of those reasons might be. We can have causes that sound very similar; it doesn't matter. Getting those possible causes out into the public arena, for collective group examination, is the important thing.

If you're working alone, you can push yourself to think of new ideas by writing your causes on a flip chart or a marking board-some place where you can see your ideas in big letters. We learn best through our eyes; so let your eyes have a place to do their best work.

If you have the good fortune to have others helping you, encourage them to share their ideas. This is brainstorming, so set a time limit, say 5 minutes. If you're the facilitator, tell the group: "we want to get as many cause ideas on the charts as possible. Don't edit yourself. Say anything that comes to mind."

Be sure to appoint someone as your sticky note manager. Write each cause suggestion from your brainstorming session on your flip chart. As you do this, your sticky-note person should put each of these cause statements on a single sticky note. The sticky notes are one of the most powerful resources within 3-D Problem-Solving. They give us the ability to move our ideas around, putting them into an infinite combination of groupings, much like the colored squares on a Rubic's Cube. Then we can break these groupings into further sub-groupings, as our analysis unfolds. We'll see how this works as Brandi and her group work their way through our Case Study.

Don't be alarmed if the number of potential causes grows to several dozen. Through the magic of sticky notes, you'll be able to package these into related groupings that can be managed efficiently.

We can use an example to demonstrate the power of groupings. Try this with a couple of friends. Ask them to name 30 different kinds of dog breeds. On a flip chart, write down each of their suggestions. Time how long it takes them to get to 30.

Now ask your friends to name 30 different kinds of birds. Only this time, write categories on your flip chart paper, such as:

- Exotic jungle birds

- Household pets

- Raptors

- Scavengers

- Food birds

- Big birds

- Tiny birds

Then work through each of the groups. Chart the responses and time how long it takes to get to 30. We suspect that the group gets to 30 much more quickly by using bird categories as a guide.

Suppose, along the same lines, that you want to brainstorm solutions to your top-priority causes. You will probably get a lot of suggestions. These, like your causes, will be far easier to manage when you put them into related groupings. For one thing, the groupings may help you to avoid duplication, as similar solution recommendations inevitably come together in your grouping process.

All that will come later. For now, all we want you to do in this step is to get your ideas onto flip chart sheets and on sticky notes so we can begin working with them.

Step Three: Sort Things Out

In this step, the sticky note monitor simply slaps all cause-statement notes randomly on one or more sheets of flip chart paper.

This done, every team member is encouraged to arrange the cause notes into related groupings, with a minimum of at least three groups, although more can be formed as needed. Everyone needs to participate--each perspective is valuable. Anyone can move any cause note to any group at any time. Anyone can discuss why he or she thinks a note should be moved to one group or another. The official name for this is "affinity sorting." We just call it "making groups."

So why do we ask you to create at least three groupings. That's so you have to push yourselves to really think about the causes and how they relate. There's obviously no gain if you only have one group—you stay right where you started. Two groups are only slightly better than one and represent little gain for whatever effort you and your colleagues expended. With three groups, people's brain cells work harder.

Talking is important during this sorting and grouping process. That's when you and your colleagues start coming to terms with the complexity of the problem and its origins. As facilitator for the group, watch out that this step in the process doesn't become a gripe session or otherwise get out of hand. As long as the sticky notes are moving around, talking is your friend.

If you're working alone, still push yourself to find natural relationships among the various causes. Discipline yourself to form at least three groups, more if needed.

Once you and your colleagues are satisfied with your groupings, draw a boundary line around each of the sets of causes. This is so you can readily tell where one groups ends and another begins.

Finally, you'll need to agree on a one to three word name for each of your groups. Don't force the groupings. Let people play with the notes. The natural instincts of humans to seek out and establish relationships among seemingly diverse ideas will do the rest.

At the end of this step you will have one or more sheets of flipchart paper, displaying three or more groupings of cause sticky notes.

Around each of the groups will be a boundary line and each group will have a distinguishing title.

Now we're ready for Step Three, prioritizing our groups so we can determine where to focus our problem-solving energy first.

Step Four: Prioritize

When fixing problems, a critical rule is that "you can't do everything at once." To be effective, 3-D problem solvers have to pick their shots, taking on first only those groups of causes that will give them the most immediate return for their efforts. Once you have implemented solutions for your top-rated problems, you can go back to your next highest-level priority, and so on until you have addressed all the causes you identified in Step 2.

The first step in prioritizing is to establish selection criteria. These provide a framework around the group's decision making, or your individual decision making if you are working alone. The criteria help focus peoples' thinking. Also, if someone asks how you arrived at the choices you did, you can always say that your choices were based on several visual, reproducible, mutually agreed-upon selection criteria.

Over the years the criteria we provide below have tended to be the ones most often chosen, so we suggest that you consider using them, at least as your core criteria.   Then, by all means, remove any that don't work for your group or situation, and add new ones that work for you:

If we remove these causes, we will have the greatest potential to:

- *Contribute to increased customer satisfaction/future sales*

- *Save the company money*

- *Save workforce time Contribute to the resolution of other cause groups or other work place problems*

Each team member is now given three votes, with votes cast at all times on the basis of the decision criteria. Each participant can cast:

- One vote on each of three cause groups

- Two votes on one cause group, one vote on another

- All three votes on one cause group

Why three votes? No particular scientific reason. It just seems to us that one or two votes doesn't allow enough latitude of decision making for each participant, and much more than three votes per person gets to be a pretty big counting chore. Have more votes per person if you like, but remember that the more votes people have the longer it will take to cast them and the more votes you'll have to count.

This "multi-voting" process helps team members spread out their concerns over a variety of causes while also disciplining them to commit to some causes over others, again always based on the criteria the group has selected.

Selecting a top-priority cause group is only the start of the process. Now that you have your top-priority group of causes, and lots of other possible causes lying in the wings, you have to dig deeper and bring greater focus to your work.

But remember, this is 3-D problem solving so we don't just grab at the first ideas that come along. We still need to do some digging.

So, whether you're working alone or in a group, take the sticky notes from your top-priority group and put them onto a fresh, blank flip chart sheet. Spread them out so everyone can see them. If there were a lot of cause notes in your top-priority cause group, you might want to sort these sticky notes into at least three additional, sub-categories. If there are only a half dozen or so cause notes, go ahead and do your multi-voting on specific cause notes.

Using the same Selection Criteria, everyone has three votes again, to cast in the same manner as earlier: all three on one cause, two on one and one on another, or one on each of three. But now everyone is voting for specific causes from within the top-priority cause group.

This will result in selection of a specific single cause to zero in on. Don't worry if this seems too limiting, especially since we have our "Rubic's Cube" of other people and process causes looming over our work.

Trust the process to get you through *all* the causes, but in an orderly manner that assures proper attention to all facets, or colors, of the Rubic's Cube.

Step Five: Find the Root Cause

The 3-D approach to problem solving tries to take as much of the guess work as possible out of fixing things that go wrong in the work place. We've already learned that the obvious causes of problems may not be so obvious at all. Now our process requires that you dig deeper. This shouldn't be too hard, or too time-consuming, if you stick with the process we outline here.

By this time, you've identified multiple causes of the defined problem, put these causes into manageable groups, prioritized the groups, using clear decision criteria, and prioritized the leading potential cause from your top-priority group.

Finding root cause requires little more than further development of causes, but specifically for this single, top-priority cause of your difficulties. Repeat Steps 2 through 4, specifically for this number-one cause. Brainstorm what might be causing this part of the problem. You'll be amazed at the further number of gremlins you smoke out this way.

Once these additional sub-causes, all focused on what you decided earlier was the top-priority cause of your problem, are on the flip charts, and transcribed onto sticky notes, you'll want to organize them into groupings. All you are doing is repeating the process steps from earlier, only this time with a much tighter focus. If questions arise that need data to answer, make it an action step in your implementation plan to get that data.

Finding root cause can be extremely satisfying; especially for a problem that has been a thorn in everyone's side for months or even years. An easy and extremely useful tool for finding root cause in hurry is to "ask why five times." A mainstay in the world of total quality control, this technique can quickly take you to what's really going on. Here's an example:

Suppose you're a supervisor in a factory and you spot a small puddle of oil on the shop floor. The puddle is only the size of a silver dollar, but you're still concerned. Viewed from a humanitarian standpoint, someone could slip on the oil and hurt themselves, causing needless pain to a fellow employee, and also leaving the company vulnerable to potential legal action or to a workers' compensation claim. From a purely process-management standpoint, oil belongs in the lubricating systems of your production machinery, not on the floor.

If you take a 2-D approach to problem solving, you might just call someone over to the oil spot and tell them to clean it up and keep it clean. If you lean toward Attila the Hun school of management, you might also chew out a few people for poor housekeeping and threaten to punish workers in the area if the oil shows up again. That might put a crew of cleaners and sweepers on high alert for a while, at considerable cost to the organization, and it might keep the oil off the floor. But the drip, drip, drip would continue.

Since you're now a 3-D problem solver, you take a more in-depth approach. As a complete pragmatist, you know that oil belongs inside the machining system not on the floor and that if you don't isolate and repair the root cause, the problem will simply continue.

So you call over a couple of fellow employees and begin asking "why" five times, starting with the obvious:

"1. *Why* (you ask): is this small puddle of oil on the floor?"

"*Because* (the employees closest to the problem reply): it is leaking from that gearbox just above the walkway."

"2. *Why:* is the oil leaking from the gearbox?

"*Because:* a gasket has cracked."

"3. *Why:* has the gasket cracked?

"*Because:* preventive maintenance wasn't performed on schedule."

"4. *Why:* wasn't preventive maintenance performed on schedule?"

"*Because:* the preventive maintenance coordinator has been out on sick leave for three weeks and no one has been doing his scheduling job."

"5. *Why:* hasn't anyone been doing his scheduling job?"

"*Because:* no one thought to designate someone to take over this responsibility in his absence."

Game, set, match, as they say at the end of a tennis competition. In an exchange that might, at most, take five minutes you have flushed out the following information about that offending oil spot:

1. The errant oil is coming from a leaking seal in a gearbox above a walkway where dozens of people pass by every day as potential injury victims.

2. Preventive maintenance, critical for long-term performance and cost savings, has been deficient in this area.

3. The person responsible for scheduling such PM is out sick and no one has been designated to manage this important responsibility.

4. The root cause of the problem isn't an oil leak but rather a personnel issue.

5. Who knows what other preventive maintenance problems, with attendant potential liability and repair costs, are lurking in that part of the plant that you haven't heard about—*yet*.

So what's the solution? Pretty simple. Ask the group to work out a permanent corrective action that includes designating someone to take care of the absent employee's preventive-maintenance scheduling.

You don't always have to ask "why" five times. Sometimes you get to root cause in only one or two "whys." Use your good judgment to determine when you've gotten to the bottom of the situation.

Keep working on Step 5 in the 3-D Problem Solving Process until the group is satisfied that you have *really* isolated what's going on within that particular top-priority cause. It may seem like you're focusing too hard on this one single cause, to the exclusion of all those many other causes you identified earlier. Don't worry. The process will get to them in short order. Trust the process, Mr. Spock, and you too will live long and prosper.

Step Six: Create Solutions

Up to this point you've been analyzing the problem, and breaking it down into readily manageable pieces. Now you're ready to take action to make the worst causes of the problem go away by identifying solutions and establishing an action plan to assure that those solutions are implemented.

Remember, we're still focusing only on solutions for the specific sub-causes of the top-priority cause of our problem. We'll get to all those other causes soon.

In our process, finding and agreeing on solutions also requires brainstorming, but of a highly focused nature. We're looking for creative ideas that have the most potential to make the root-cause of our problem go away—if not permanently, as close to it as possible.

We use the same charting system, with a sticky note manager putting each solution idea on its own separate note. We also bundle our ideas into related groupings, like we did with our cause notes. Only this time we group our solutions around the specific causes they are intended to remedy.

If there are concerns about being able to implement all the solutions right away, you may want to prioritize them, again using our Decision Criteria and multi-voting. Otherwise, just post your Solutions and move on to action planning.

So how do we know our recommended solutions will work? In all honesty, we don't know for sure. But we have the collective wisdom of the problem-solving group backing up our conclusions. We also have the capability to build monitoring and measuring systems into our implementation plan so we can constantly check the efficacy of our solutions. If things are improving the way we want them to, we continue. If they aren't, we make the necessary adjustments.

The 3-D Problem-Solving Process gives us that level of flexibility.

Step Seven: Check Results and Repeat the Process

Here's where the process helps you get maximum mileage out of your first round of solutions.

Before taking on each cause grouping and individual cause, take the solutions you crafted for your top-priority cause and see what other problems they eliminate. The recurring magic is that by focusing intently on a single root cause, you end up fixing several other causes. These turn out to be related to each other, even though it was considerably less than obvious when you first examined the problem.

You'll be pleasantly surprised at the results of this exercise. Mark each of the cause notes that are swept into the vortex of your first set of solutions and moves them over to the work area for your top-priority cause.

Now you can go to your next highest-priority cause grouping, pull the individual cause notes out, place them on a blank piece of chart paper and start doing your root cause analysis again. Develop solutions for these causes, check back to see what additional causes are captured, and continue the process until you have solutions addressing each of your original cause statements.

Step Eight: Create a "Bullet-Proof" Action Plan

You've done good work until now, defining the problem, identifying causes, organizing and prioritizing causes and creating solutions. But none of this is of any earthly value if your solutions aren't implemented successfully. The 3-D Problem-Solving Process is all about application; otherwise, why do it!

But it's not enough to simply work out a plan and hope for the best. We want to do everything to assure that our plan works.

Here's how we "bullet-proof" our action plan.

Either you as an individual, or with your work group, need to assign specific "action items" to be achieved for each solution.

Each action item should be captured on a sticky note and should say:

- *Who* is responsible

- For *what* action

- To be *completed* by what date

It's essential to assign a specific individual to a specific action, with a completion date attached. Otherwise there's a strong likelihood that that action will never be completed. The person assigned responsibility for a specific task doesn't necessarily have to personally do that task. He or she simply needs to make sure that it gets done on time, or if problems arise, that additional time and resources are acquired as needed.

Further Bullet-Proofing Your Action Plan

Further bulletproofing your action plan requires nothing more than sensible risk management. Wise project planners always take time to assess what might go wrong and to decide what they will do if any of these "worst-case" situations occur.

Once all your action items have been posted in their order of completion, take time by yourself or with your group and ask:

"What can go wrong with this plan?"

This question will generate a list of possible problems that can slow down or halt implementation of your solution plans. Chart this list, then go back and, for each risk, ask:

- *What can we do to prevent this risk from happening?*

- *What can we do if, despite our prevention efforts, this risk occurs anyway?*

The answers to these two questions will generate additional action items. Note them as you would any other action, with a responsible person identified, the action clarified, and the completion date established. This "crystal ball" approach will help you head off a lot of "show stoppers," such as senior-management resistance or sudden lack of funds.

The time you spend on "bullet-proofing" will pay off handsomely.

Once all your action items have been posted in their order of completion, take time by yourself or with your group and ask:

"What can go wrong with this plan?"

This question will generate a list of possible problems that can slow down or halt implementation of your solution plans. Chart this list, then go back and for each risk, ask:

- *What can we do to prevent this risk from happening?*

- *What can we do if, despite our prevention efforts, this risk occurs anyway?*

The answers to these two questions will generate additional action items. Note them as you would any other action, with a responsible person identified, the action clarified, and the completion date established. This "crystal ball" approach will help you head off a lot of "show stoppers," such as senior-management resistance or sudden lack of funds. The time you spend on "bullet-proofing" will pay off handsomely.

Step Ten: Teaching the Process

Assuming you like what you've read so far, you will want to expose others to this way of tackling problems. The more people who are familiar with these techniques the more support you will have in analyzing and overcoming problems in ways that get predictably positive results.

Good luck in putting the Lone Ranger out of business.

What we've done up to now has hopefully been informative and maybe even a bit entertaining. But that's not good enough in today's work place environment. You need real world results.

We're sure there's no shortage of problems at your work place. Pick out a particularly bothersome one, assemble a small group of colleagues, brief them on the 3-D approach, and give them this book to read, get yourself a flip chart and some sticky notes and take it for a spin.

NOTES

Chapter 8

Building Powerful Teams And Groups For Problem Solving: Without The "Lone Ranger"

As we said many times earlier, the Lone Ranger is too often on the loose in the American work place, today as in those thrilling days of yesteryear, and he's causing lots of trouble. This is nowhere more evident than in the creation and management of work groups and teams.

It's evident from the previous chapter that the finding and permanent solution of core work-place problems, a fundamental if the kaizen/ISO Cash Machine, takes time. How much time varies based on such things as problem and solution complexity, team problem-solving skills and leadership support. The payoff is that, once corrected using kaizen techniques, such problems tend to stay solved, at considerable savings of time and money for the organization.

Unfortunately, the organizational pressure often remains to not "waste time" analyzing problem situations, especially when one or more senior "veterans" know exactly what to do. After all they've seen "this kind of thing before." Of course they've seen it before—it's been a recurring problem, like those defective up-scale auto engines that never got built right in the first place.

In today's pressure-cooker business environment a speedy, can-do dynamic can look mighty appealing. It fits the American business psyche, where the cry too often is to "do something," even if— oops—that "something" ultimately creates more confusion than enlightenment. It's the "ready, fire, aim" syndrome run amok.

What sustains all those Lone Rangers on the job, it seems, is that every now then one of their "silver bullets" actually hits a worthy target.

Unfortunately, also, most of their hip shots simply cause otherwise helpful bystanders, willing workers all, to duck for cover as the latest corporate "super star" shows his or her prowess at "getting things done around here."

We see some of the most profound negative impact of the Lone Ranger mentality in the creation and management of work groups and teams. As you can see in our chapter on problem solving, finding permanent corrective solutions to the root causes of problems takes a bit more than a few "hip shots," tossed off at random because "something has to be done."

That these modern-day masked avengers may make things worse too often goes unnoticed. By the time the quick-fix band-aids of your average corporate Lone Ranger have finally come unraveled, the super star has, like his masked role model, moved on to another desperate problem, and another and another.

Alas, in too many organizations the Lone Rangers among us are likely to get promoted for their gun-slinging prowess, while it remains for practitioners of less spectacular, if more substantive, problem-solving techniques to clean up after these "heroes." (It's the same principle that applies when sweepers clean up after an equestrian parade—silver-bedecked horses and flamboyant riders bask in the applause and acclaim; the clean-up crews handle the....well you get the idea.)

The painful irony in this saga of the Long Ranger run amok in American companies is that a well-formed team, using the right techniques, can work just as fast as the masked man—often faster when you factor in that inevitable clean-up detail.

We want to knock the Lone Rangers of American business off their high silver horses. Our mini-crusade is to <u>show</u> the destructiveness of lone-gun problem solving in action, and to contrast this with the relative ease, and substantial benefits, of taking time to let a well-developed team get the job done right.

Our simple contention is that powerful and effective work place teams aren't that hard to create and sustain—no harder than forming a good posse in the old west. Just pick the right people, put them through a few simple planning steps, then put them to work catching the bad guys. All we require is that you complete the planning steps, <u>every time</u>.

Having sent the Lone Ranger packing, at least for now, let's get down to the task of making powerful kaizen/ISO problem-solving work groups and teams.

First let's define what we mean by "work group" and "team" in the context of kaizen/ISO problem solving and permanent corrective action.

Small Groups Defined

We consider a "small" work group or team as having from three to fifteen members.   Two people, working together, don't have nearly the same kinds of challenges as those faced by three or more. Make the group too large, and it will tend to break up into sub groups, which may or may not compete with one another. The management techniques for these larger groups are also very different and more formal than the types of human combinations we propose that you work with in kaizen/ISO problem solving.

Steven A. Beebe, et. al., in their book *Communicating for a Lifetime—Communicating in Small Groups and Teams,* offer a definition of small groups that allows us to examine several of the important elements of the subject. They write that:

> "A small group consists of three to fifteen people who share a <u>common purpose</u>, who feel a <u>sense of belonging</u> to the group, and who <u>exert influence</u> on one another."

Please take careful note of the phrase "common purpose." We will revisit this concept frequently in studying how groups go awry and how they can be renewed. For now, let's just agree that when three to fifteen people have a common purpose they can be considered a small group.

As Beebe explains, "a collection of people waiting for an elevator may all want to go somewhere, but they probably haven't organized their efforts so that they are going to the same place." Groups, on the other hand, make concerted efforts to "organize" themselves around a common objective. This sense of common purpose can lead to a further sense of "belonging" for members, that they are indeed working together to achieve their common purpose.

The Nature of Work Groups and Teams

Before going further, it's useful for us to determine the difference between groups and teams. It's easy to use the terms group and team interchangeably. In fact, there are critical differences between the two.

Most of the scholarly thinking on this subject deals with levels of coordination. Group members, as we have seen, are committed to achieving a common purpose. But members of groups don't ordinarily spend as much time as team members in developing strong levels of bonding and of devotion to achieving goals as effectively as possible.

On teams, care is taken to assure that the most qualified members are assigned to specific tasks. This is especially so on sports teams. Moreover, on teams each member's duties are carefully spelled out. With so much specialization, it is also important that team members know exactly how they will operate together. Misdirected energy in this area can readily waste time, money and emotions. On groups, but more so on teams, behavior must be clearly defined. We'll take a closer look at this concept.

Our approach to group/team development and management applies equally to both of these configurations, freeing you up to apply our approaches for an ad hoc work group with a clearly defined yet limited purpose or for a more permanent problem-solving or project team.

We've been around organizational work group and team development for lots of years. Our recommendations here are a synthesis of the things we learned over the years into a simple and highly compressed series of concepts and steps.

How's this for basic? We think three small words can set you on the road to forming and running effective problem-solving groups/teams. Those words are:

- What

- Who

- How

Let's take a closer look at each of them, starting with "what."

What

Too often, leaders don't effectively communicate to group members what the goal or goals are for their unified efforts. Members often don't know precisely what they are expected to achieve or deliver. In fact, sometimes there isn't even clear explanation of the group's reason for existence.

A group may be called the "Strategy Team," or the "Future Products and Services Team," or whatever, and it may have been introduced to the organization with lots of hoopla and fanfare. But a flashy name or lots of publicity won't do much to clarify what the group is supposed to accomplish or what the specific, and we emphasize specific, responsibilities are for group leaders and individual members.

Not surprisingly, most such groups often sputter and die, with accompanying decline in morale and company resources. Time, money and motivation have been squandered on yet another foray into the murky world of small groups.

From the outset, clearly defining the group/team's essential objective, the "what." is critical. Clear group goals drive all subsequent decisions, including who will be in the group, how well the group can be expected to embrace the principles of group effectiveness, what will be measured and how it will be done, and the boundaries of group empowerment.

Without clear goals, team members won't know how to apply their abilities. Group effectiveness suffers. Team members won't know what to measure because they won't know where the group should be going.

"Clear Goals" is exactly what it says, a clear rendering of <u>what</u> the group or team members are expected to produce. Group/ team creators, and other stakeholders, need to provide abundant opportunity for members to ask clarification questions about what they are there to accomplish.

To do the best job, everyone connected with the project will need to form commitment to these goals and be sure that others share these same objectives and levels of commitment. Questioning and listening techniques are important here, for members and for those with a professional stake in group/team success.

We're fans of the "SMART" approach to goal clarification. Within the SMART system, a group/team goal should fulfill the following requirements:

Specific: A specific goal has a much greater chance of being accomplished than a general goal. To set a specific goal you must answer, for example, such questions as:

- Who is involved?

- What is to be accomplished?

- Where will the work take place?

- When are the start and finish times?

- Why is this work being pursued, the specific reasons, purposes or benefits of accomplishing the goal?

Here's an example: A too-general goal would be, "Get in shape." But a specific goal would say, "Join a health club and work out three days a week until my weight has gone down 20 pounds, my blood pressure is in the normal range and my clothes fit better."

Measurable: Establish concrete criteria for measuring progress toward the attainment of each goal you set. When you measure your progress, you stay on track, reach your target dates, and experience the exhilaration of achievement that spurs you on to continued effort required to reach your goal.

To determine if your goal is measurable, ask questions such as......How much? How many? How will I know when it is accomplished?

Attainable: When you identify goals that are most important to you, you begin to figure out ways you can make them come true. You develop the attitudes, abilities, skills, and financial capacity to reach them. You begin seeing previously overlooked opportunities to bring yourself closer to the achievement of your goals.

You can attain most any goal you set when you plan your steps wisely and establish a time frame that allows you to carry out those steps. Goals that may have seemed far away and out of reach eventually move closer and become attainable, not because your goals shrink, but because you grow and expand to match them. When you list your goals you build your self-image. You see yourself as worthy of these goals, and develop the traits and personality that allow you to possess them.

Realistic: To be realistic, a goal must represent an objective toward which you are both *willing* and *able* to work. A goal can be both high and realistic; you are the only one who can decide just how high your goal should be. But be sure that every goal represents substantial progress.

A lofty goal is frequently easier to reach than a low one because a low goal exerts low motivational force. Some of the hardest jobs you ever accomplished may have actually seemed easy simply because they were a labor of love.

Your goal is probably realistic if you truly *believe* that it can be accomplished. Additional ways to know if your goal is realistic is to determine if you have accomplished anything similar in the past or ask yourself what conditions would have to exist to accomplish this goal.

Time Bound: A goal should be grounded within a time frame. With no time frame tied to it there's no sense of urgency. If you want to lose 10 pounds, when do you want to lose it by? "Someday" won't work. But if you anchor it within a timeframe, "by May 1st", then you've set your unconscious mind in motion to begin working on the goal, measuring progress along the way.

Now that we know more about the "What" phase of group/team building let's look at the "Who," determination of what people will be involved in making our goal or goals happen.

Who

Once you, as the group/team leader or sponsor, are clear on the purpose of the group—what it is intended to do, you'll need to decide who the right people are to get the job done.

There are lots of criteria that you can use in selecting the right candidates for group/team membership, from influence in the organization to advanced skills in the group's focus area.

For now, let's say that you should keep at least two macro considerations in mind in your selections, each of them in our opinion having equal importance.

One is professional expertise. Does the candidate have the skills to contribute effectively to the group and its objectives?

The second question is this: Does the candidate have the interpersonal and group/team-member abilities to operate effectively in the group environment. All groups and teams are different, day to day and through their lifetimes. Putting someone in a group because he/she has a particular skill, but with little or even negative group-participation ability, can seriously threaten effectiveness.

Now that we've clarified what the group/team exists to do, and who will do it, let's look at "How" we will go about operating our group/team.

How

There's plenty of information out there on the care and feeding of groups in the work place. True to our earlier commitments, we want to keep our recommendations basic and practical. For that, let's start with a simple model of how groups and teams evolve.

Group/Team Evolution Model

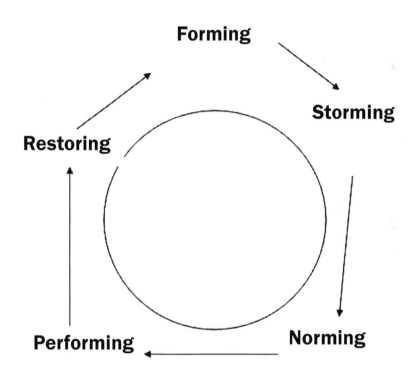

We'll offer our group/team operating instructions in the context of this construct—what we call the Group/Team Evolution Model. This is an old war horse within the world of organizational development; something often called the "Orming Model" because four of the five evolution steps end with the letters "orming."

Forming

We start at the "forming" stage, with members being careful to behave well with their team mates. Here are some examples:

In the "Forming" stage, members:

- Are careful to behave well with each other

- Try to avoid saying the wrong thing

- Present responses during discussions that appear to be tentative and somewhat unsure

- Aren't sure how they "fit in" to the group; what they can contribute or if their contributions are of value

- Aren't sure about the goals and purposes of their group

The forming stage of a group/team is seldom very productive, so it is important to move away from it as quickly as possible. From the forming stage, groups predictably move into the "storming" stage.

Storming

After the forming stage, a certain amount of conflict "storming" can be expected as group members challenge each other, and in many cases, also confront the group leaders.

In the "Storming" stage, members:

- Begin challenging each other

- Openly disagree with group leaders

- Appear aggravated if they don't get their way

- Question their place in the group

- Question the group's general purposes and reason to exist

As tempting as it may seem to try skipping this stage, we don't recommend it. Group/team members need a certain amount of conflict with one another to build solidarity, so long as things don't get out of control.

The issue here isn't so much that the "storming" stage is bypassed, but rather how long it lasts. Does the group/team become hopelessly mired in bickering and dysfunction? Or are there a few interpersonal "flare-ups," followed by shared commitment to achieving shared goals?

Establishing answers to these questions is a function of the "norming" stage, the next stage of our model.

Norming

After the "storming" stage comes "norming," in which group/team members begin to agree on how they will behave with each other. Here also is where training in problem-solving, conflict-management and other kaizen/ISO skills is provided. A communication plan is established, with clear identification of key "target-audience stakeholders.

In the "Norming" stage, members:

- Begin to agree on group outcomes

- Clarify why the group should exist

- Determine what each member can contribute

- Establish how members will communicate and behave with each other in order to get top output

- Openly discuss what is working, what can be improved and how such improvements should be made

- Agree, either verbally or in writing, about how the group should do its work

It is during the norming stage that "ground rules" are established to manage interpersonal behavior. Let's take a closer look at ground rules before moving on to the performing and restoring stages of our model.

The forming stage of the model can be unnecessarily prolonged when group members aren't sure how they should behave with each other. We want to get through the storming stage as quickly as possible so the group/team can move on to performing, where productive work is getting done.

One way to do this, at the outset of storming, is to establish group/team ground rules, agreed standards of behavior to be adhered to be each group member. Members should participate in developing these ground rules for themselves so they have a vested interest in their use.

After conducting hundreds of ground-rules development sessions, we have found that most groups feel members should:

- Respect each other

- Listen to each other

- Participate fully in group activities

- Communicate honestly

- Give and receive trust

One of the most important objectives of ground rules are to establish a group climate of trust, support and cohesiveness. Judy Pearson, et. al., in their book *Human Communication,* define "trust" as a means for members "to believe they can rely on each other." Such reliance implies the existence of an atmosphere of openness and mutual concern. Cohesiveness means members feel "attachment toward each other and the group." Such groups "are more open, handle disagreement more effectively, and typically perform better than non-cohesive groups."

Performing

"Norms" of behavior and operation provide the structure needed for consistently high levels of group/team achievement within the next stage of our model, "performing."

In the "Performing" stage, members:

- Seek and often achieve consistently achieve high-quality work

- Monitor performance, seeking improvements where necessary

- Acknowledge each other's contributions

- Visibly support group objectives and seek creative ways to achieve them

- Take pride in group accomplishments

Using our approach to the building of ad hoc problem-solving work groups or more permanent continuous-improvement teams, leaders can reasonably expect to see high performance results.

Training in a consistent and effective problem-solving process, along with clear mutual goals, behavioral "norms" through ground rules, along with appropriate measurement and accountability systems, helps group/team members literally "know what I am supposed to do."

Restoring

Groups and teams are sensitive organisms that react to change, whether it's the entry or departure of members, changes in group goals or work assignments, or addition or departure of key internal or external stakeholders.

In the "Restoring" stage, members:

- Celebrate the contributions of someone who is leaving the group

- Celebrate the arrival of someone who is joining the group

- Acknowledge the sadness and sense of loss that members may feel at the departure of a trusted colleague

- Make new arrivals feel welcome and aware of how the group operates

The question for leaders of kaizen organizations regarding group/ team changes is not "will change impact the group/team?" We know there will be an impact. The question is "how will the change impact the group/team?" Will the group spin into an uncontrolled return to the storming stage of the evolution process? Or will the group/team simply acknowledge the change, routinely process its implications and quickly return to "performing."

To avoid the challenge of uncontrolled change and its potential negative impact on performance, we recommend that the group/ team have processes in place for "restoration" of equilibrium when changes arrive.

These may be little more than systems for celebrating the contributions of departing members and for orienting new members to group/team goals, behavior standards and operating procedures.

A Final Note on Groups/Teams and Kaizen

The group/team development and management systems we offer here have worked effectively for our kaizen/continuous improvement work for many years. They can also work for you in building and operating your Cash Machine.

In other words, the techniques for kaizen teaming and problem solving aren't especially complex, expensive, or time consuming, so long as you put them into place and use them consistently.

Chapter 9

Communicating For Dollars
In the "Cash-Machine" Organization

Communication is the life blood of your Cash Machine organization.

With enlightened, well-planned communication, keyed to the basics of kaizen/continuous improvement, your Cash Machine has strong potential to thrive and continue to generate, well, cash.

Eliminate or constrain communication and your Cash Machine organization will underperform and very likely get on the wrong side of the Change/Tech Curve and die.

Harsh words?

You bet.

Why do we put such heavy emphasis on the value of something as "soft" as organizational communication?

Simple.

Kaizen/continuous improvement is communication. Done right, your kaizen systems work like loud speakers, broadcasting to all involved what needs fixing, where it's broken, and what needs to be done to make things better.

Put another way, kaizen/continuous improvement is a big, organization-wide device that lets everyone listen to their work processes, understand what the processes are saying, and turn that information into cash, the "found money" that your Cash Machine's front end loader scoops up every day and puts to positive instead of negative use.

Like much else about creating your Cash Machine, effective kaizen communication isn't that hard to do. You surely don't need a lot of exotic new communication technology, surgically implanted Twitter receivers in each employee's eyeball and such. You won't need a staff of expensive communication professionals cobbling away on news releases and newsletters in some obscure corner of the headquarters building. And most merciful, employees won't need to spend hours at "communication" meetings at all levels, unburdening their souls in touchy-feely splendor while slurping company coffee and eating company muffins.

On the contrary. Such glitzy organizational communication window dressing is the very thing enlightened kaizen leaders should shun like the plague—this admonition coming primarily from Dan, a veteran of organizational communication staffs at

General Motors, Weyerhaeuser Company and other corporations, large and small. Dan has written the newsletters, watched the exotic techno-gadgetry worm its way into the corporate DNA, and marveled over the years at the waste all this can generate.

All you need to get started on good communication in a kaizen/continuous improvement organization is a <u>kaizen communication mindset</u>, a state of mind not significantly different from the basic way leaders need to think to get into the kaizen/ISO game in the first place—openness to change and commitment to always seeking better ways to do the work.

To create and lead a kaizen-driven Cash Machine, leaders must make these basic principles real, tangible and clearly understood by all members of the organization.

In the early stages of the transition process from traditional organization to kaizen/continuous improvement organization, leaders must constantly communicate about three strategic-planning questions, and do it for all employees at all levels:

1. What is kaizen/continuous improvement?

2. Why are we making the change to kaizen/continuous improvement?

3. What does the change mean for me?

The content of your answers to these questions is essentially up to you. We'll offer some suggestions here, but the details reside with each Cash Machine organization.

What is Kaizen/Continuous Improvement And Why Do We Need It?

Most of the basic information you'll need to communicate the case for a kaizen transition is in the early chapters of this book. Go back and pick out the messages that seem to work best for you.

Here are some key kaizen messages we've seen leaders use particularly well in generating understanding and commitment.

- We are going to begin adopting the principles and practices of kaizen/continuous improvement.

- This means everything we do will be subject to continuous improvement.

- We are doing this in order to stay in business; we must continually improve in all areas to stay just ahead of the competition.

- This means every employee will have the opportunity to find and implement ways to improve their work processes, whatever those may be.

- Everyone will be trained in the techniques of kaizen problem solving

- Our first step in this transition process will be to seek ISO certification.

- The ISO process will give us a quick, manageable and relatively inexpensive means of identifying our readiness to practice kaizen successfully.

- Your direct supervisors will provide continuing details of our kaizen transition process, and will welcome your questions and observations.

It will help if you have a strategic communication planning process available to use in developing your kaizen communication plan.

To do this you'll first need a clear definition of communication, one that helps you frame exactly what you want your communication system to do.

Here's one we have used effectively for many years; it's short, reasonably understandable and practical:

Human communication is a **process** during which a **source** individually initiates a **message,** using **verbal** and **nonverbal symbols** and **contextual cues** to express **meaning** by transmitting **information** in such a way that similar or parallel **understandings** are constructed by the **intended receiver(s)**.

–Margaret DeFleur, et. Al., *Fundamentals of Human Communication, 3rd edition.*

Stated another way, communication among humans happens when a source sends information to a receiver, who understands the information and acts on it as intended.

Easy to say, but not always easy to do. Here are four basic communication planning steps that can help assure that your kaizen messages are received as sent.

Step 1: Identify key internal and external audiences. Ask yourself: "who are the people who must successfully receive our messages about kaizen, during transition and afterward?"

Step 2: Identify the essential messages that each of these internal and external audiences must receive about kaizen. Ask yourself: "what are the kinds of kaizen-change messages that will best satisfy the information needs of this group?"

Step 3: Determine the best delivery system(s) to assure that each audience successfully receives its messages. This is the "media" part of the puzzle. To put this step into the context of a restaurant, remember that media, whether stories around a campfire or the latest iteration of Twitter, are never more than "trays" that carry information "dishes" to the right people at the right tables. Ask yourself: "what information delivery system will work best for this group?"

Step 4: Set up a feedback system that tells you how well members of each audience are receiving which messages. Ask yourself: "are these kaizen messages being received, and if so, what impact are they having?"

Use Step 4 to continuously improve your communication system.

And while you're seeking continuous communication improvement, don't limit yourself. Be creative. Mix verbal communication with nonverbal communication, in the form of models, pictures and other visuals.

Strive to keep things interesting and relevant. To do this you'll need to know your audience, something that happens when you get out of your office and go to where the work is being done.

And while you're there listen, listen, listen, and not just with your ears. Learn to listen with your eyes.

Okay, you may be saying about now, these guys have just stepped off the deep end.

Not so. In the world of communication there's something called "active listening." That's where the listener pays close attention to the meaning of the words being heard, not just the sounds, while at all times noting visual information—body language, physical surroundings, speaking pace and tone, and other clues.

Also, and we can't emphasize this enough. In your transition to kaizen, you're dealing with a change situation. This means there are some behavioral and communications conditions that you can reasonably anticipate.

For one, most employees won't embrace your argument for change with open arms. No matter how nurturing the culture in an organization, employees are wary of change. Their survival depends on each of them doing a "good job." Change implies that they haven't been doing a good job, so there's a tendency for them to feel defensive. Such defensiveness doesn't make for especially open receptivity to new ideas, no matter how solid the rationale.

So as you communicate the need for transition to kaizen, and the value of the ISO initiative, don't be shocked when you encounter resistance. You'll likely recognize this in vocal tones, and silences, as well as in the actual words that employees use.

Do four things when this happens:

1. Don't take it personally; it's not about you.

2. Don't react to what is said and done at kaizen/ISO information sessions, especially by over-defending kaizen or the need for it to be the operating principle of your organization.

3. Listen, listen, listen

4. Give employees time to assimilate the changes.

And persist. For this we offer the words of a GM division vice president from years ago who said of change communication:

> "You have to keep saying it over and over again. Just when you think you can't stand to repeat the same message again, is about when the employees start understanding and committing to the new ways."

Good thinking at any time.

NOTES

Chapter 10

Leading the
"Cash-Machine" Organization

Leadership of a "Cash Machine" organization relies on a handful of basic assumptions, ones that don't always align with the profit-driven gospel of modern management. Here are three that we think are especially important:

Assumption 1: go for the improvements and the money will follow.

Assumption 2: teach continuous improvement to employees and trust them to do the right thing.

Assumption 3: get out of your office and go to where the work is being done; you'll learn more that way and it will help employees trust you more.

Let's take a closer look at each of these.

Assumption 1: go for the improvements and the money will follow.

As our colleague, Max Gregorich, has made clear, the big performance numbers you want reside in the understanding and improving of work processes, not in driving for the highest profits in the short term.

The problem of focusing too much on profit is that you may get what you wish for, today and even tomorrow. But you will also risk getting that much closer to the deadly Change/Tech Curve.

That's because to make profit, at the exclusion of continuous improvement, you have to skimp on such things as employee training, budgeting of time for problem-solving teams to do their work, and communicating the reasons and techniques of kaizen.

This doesn't even take into account reductions in marketing, research and development, human resources and other vital functions. Costs go down in the short run, but the organization gets progressively more anemic until its competitiveness is jeopardized.

Put another way, shrinking costs to get short-term profits makes the organization weaker; practicing kaizen/continuous improvement makes the organization a bit stronger every business day.

You decide.

Assumption 2: teach continuous improvement to employees and trust them to do the right thing.

In some organizations, investing in employee skills can seem counter-intuitive. After all, the reasoning goes, they're doing okay now. Why spend a lot of money, and time, training them to do something else.

To which we reply, the Change/Tech Curve never sleeps. Everything changes in your industry all the time, and the only way that employees, and leaders, can adapt to these changes is to keep learning and improving, all the time.

Just like professional athletes who attend clinics, get coaching and practice, practice, practice, effective employees keep their edge by means of training sessions, coaching and practice.

Spending time and money on employee improvement isn't a cost of doing business but an investment in future survival.

Assumption 3: get out of your office and go to where the work is being done; you'll learn more that way and it will help employees trust you more.

Japanese business gurus call the process of leaders visiting the work floors "going to gemba," which means "going to where the work, and accompanying problems and solutions, is happening."

As part of "going to gemba," kaizen leaders routinely work on their listening and observing skills. In the best kaizen spirit, they recognize that everything they do as leaders can be continuously improved.

This isn't a book on leadership so we won't go into more detail on leading the kaizen organization. Just know that step one of kaizen is the decision by top leaders to make its power part of the way the organization does business.

Our colleague Max Gregorich summarizes the challenges of kaizen driven change when he writes that:

> *Once you've planned properly, stepping out of the box will become easier and more comfortable. Will it ever be completely comfortable? No, but the excitement of the game and the potential rewards will so overshadow the discomfort of taking those first steps that you won't even notice it. Once success is at hand, you probably won't remember the discomfort.*

From there, with determination and a reasonable amount of humble respect for what employees can do to make improvements when given the skills and opportunities, you can help keep your Cash Machine's name in the telephone book.

NOTES

Chapter 11

Setting Your
"Cash-Machine" Priorities

Business consultant Max Gregorich has made his living over the years helping organizations large and small find and retrieve the money that feeds your Cash Machine. We offer a few of his most compelling thoughts on kaizen/continuous improvement here. For more on Max's thinking, visit his web site at www.ceo1stop. com.

Let's start with Max's thinking on organization survival and the role of kaizen in keeping the doors open.

Max writes:

> More than 80% of businesses fail because of poor financial planning and decision making. The defeated businessperson usually cries, "I was undercapitalized." "My sales weren't great enough to generate the money I needed to get to the finish line."
>
> Well, that's the usual story. But in reality, a lack of information or understanding of the financial consequences causes poor decision making in the first place. Even if ten times the money needed were available, the business would probably still fail! You see, throwing money at the problem isn't usually a good solution.
>
> The solution is the ability to understand the information contained in the business financials and to make sound decisions based on that understanding.

In other words, says Max, you can't buy your way around kaizen/ continuous improvement. You have to "wire your work processes for sound," as we noted earlier. If you don't know what's going on in your work processes and in your decision making "ten times the money," spent blindly would still likely result in failure.

So how does Max explain this seemingly illogical assertion? How can spending more money lead to diminishing results?

Max explains it this way:

> If you owned a company whose sales were $1MM with a 10% profit ($100,000) and you wanted to double your profits to $200,000, would you rather reduce costs by 11.11% or double your total sales?

Assume for this example that both approaches would achieve the goal of a $200,000 profit.

Most of you may have already chosen to reduce costs, but I have to say that in my financial analysis workshops, slightly more than half the people I speak to choose to double their sales. This tells me that most small and mid-sized business owners still think that the top line (net sales) is the answer to their bottom line (net profit) worries.

But if they both get you to the same goal, a $200,000 profit, what's the difference? Let's analyze both answers.

What will it take to double your sales? You may have to add the costs of doubling your marketing, advertising, and sales efforts; double your staff, which may include doubling the size of your facility; double the equipment needed -- you get the idea.

And to top it off, you, as the business owner, will have to manage an organization that's now twice its original size. Since you're now probably working only 14 to 18 hour days, working twice as long shouldn't be a problem.

Right?

Now let's look at cutting your costs by 11.11%. All the costs associated with doubling your sales instantly go away.

You may, though, need to invest some time in analyzing your costs to determine where you can reduce them. You may have to invest some money to fix some problems. In the end, you'll probably find that you're over staffed for your current net sales. If this is the case, you'll also find that your facility is larger than necessary; you have more equipment than you need -- again, you get the idea.

The next thing you know, you're managing less and have still doubled your bottom line. Here comes the best part: Now that your work day has been reduced to something much less than 18 hours, you'll see that **reducing internal costs has the added benefit of enabling you to beat your competition in the market place if you wish to do so.**

Now that it's cheaper for you to deliver your product or service to the customer, you may wish to consider lowering your prices to gain market share while still enjoying greater profit, leaving your competitors to wonder how you do it. Since you're not in the business of laying off your employees, you can clearly see the benefit of increased market share. Those extra people you didn't need are now earning you more profits and increasing your top line simultaneously.

In the end, if properly executed, your cost reduction project ends up increasing your bottom line to something greater than the originally planned $200,000 because you also found a way to increase your top line.

The lesson? Internal cost reduction and market penetration must be carried out simultaneously if you want growth. This absolutely bears repeating: **If you want real growth, you must always strive to reduce your costs and increase market share simultaneously.**

And what is one of the most reliable ways to reduce costs? Kaizen/continuous improvement. By adopting kaizen, you will have implemented Max's cost-cutting recommendations, no as an episodic gain or two but as a never-ending way of organizational life. You will have created a Cash Machine.

Max sees the capturing of those otherwise wasted dollars from recurring process problems and ill-advised leadership decisions as relatively simple endeavors:

> If my 20 years as a business consultant have taught me anything, it's that cost reduction is fairly straight forward and there is usually plenty of low hanging fruit. About 90% of the companies I've visited could easily at least double their bottom line with very little investment of time and money.
>
> But I've also learned that most small and mid-sized business owners do not have the financial training to do the necessary analysis. Where do you look? How do you find the pit that's consuming the profits? This book can help you discover the way.
>
> Most small business owners use "cigar box accounting" -- money coming in this month minus the money going out this month equals profit or loss -- and that's the extent of it. When your tax returns are prepared at the end of the year, you learn the real truth.

At this point Max asks a series of survival-level questions, ones every organizational leader should ponder as he or she works to keep the organization away from the deadly Change/Tech Curve:

> "If you were profitable, great. But do you know why you were profitable?
>
> If you weren't profitable, it's too late to do anything about it. More importantly: Do you know why you weren't profitable?
>
> What could you have done if you'd had the necessary information earlier?

Remember, you can't fix the past -- only the future. Look what happened to Enron when they tried to fix the past. So the sooner you get the information and interpret it, the sooner you can fix the future.

In other words, the longer you wait the more money you lose. Lose enough and you're out of business and become one of those "statistics" business professors talk about in their classrooms.

Now we're getting to the crux of the matter -- If you'd only had the information sooner!

For Max, the universal lament of decision makers is "if I'd only had the information earlier!"

The tragedy, as we noted earlier, is that the information needed for money-saving decision making, the kind of decision making that drives your Cash Machine, was there all the time.

"Perhaps you didn't know you had it," Max says. "Perhaps you knew you had it but didn't know how to interpret it. Perhaps you didn't know how to fix the root cause of the problem."

The information you need can be readily found in "your bookkeeping software, your ledgers, or your tax returns." In other words, it's hidden in plain sight.

Then, says Max, "it's up to you to interpret these statements."

Max offers a model of such a statement and discusses how to interpret it for Cash Machine savings:

Income Statement:

Period: January 1 through December 31, 20xx   Values are in Dollars

	Sales	3,787,179
Direct Costs		
	Materials	936,491
	Labor	644,226
	Subcontractors	101,098
	Other Direct	1,044,284
		————
Cost of Goods Sold		2,736,099
		————
Gross Profit		1,061,080
Indirect Costs		
	Sales Salaries	252,378
	Advertising/ Promotion	36,852
	Distribution/ Transportation	24,001
	Repairs and Maintenance	8,456
	Other Indirect	63,869
	Total Indirect	385,556
General & Administrative Costs		
	Owner's Salary	70,097
	Admin Wages	290,084
	Depreciation/ Amortization	17,799
	Interest Expense	5,838

	Facilities Expense	114,385
	Other G&A Costs	259,502
		_____
Total G&A Costs		757,705
		_____
Cost of Operations		1,143,261
		_____
Net Profit		(82,181) Losses/negative numbers are in parentheses.)

In a vertical analysis, says Max, "you create a ratio between every individual line item and the Net Sales (Sales) value in percentage." It looks like this:

	Sales (Net Sales)	**3,787,179**	**100%**
Direct Costs			
	Materials	936,491	24.7%
	Labor	644,226	17.0%
	Subcontractors	101,098	2.7%
	Other Direct	1,044,284	27.6%
		————	
Cost of Goods Sold (total Direct Costs) Also known as COGS		2,736,099	72.0%
		————	
Gross Profit (Sales minus COGS)	1,061,080		28.0%
Indirect Costs			
	Sales Salaries	252,378	6.7%
	Advertising/ Promotion	36,852	1.0%
	Distribution/ Transportation	24,001	0.6%
	Repairs and Maintenance	8,456	0.2%
	Other Indirect	63,869	1.7%
		————	
	Total Indirect	385,556	10.2%
General & Administrative Costs			
	Owner's Salary	70,097	1.9%
	Admin Wages	290,084	7.7%

Depreciation/ Amortization	17,799	0.5%
Interest Expense	5,838	0.2%
Facilities Expense	114,385	3.0%
Other G&A Costs	259,502	6.9%

Total G&A Costs	757,705	20.0%
Cost of Operations	1,143,261	30.2%

(Total G&A + Total Indirect)

Net Profit	(82,181)	-2.2% Loss (Gross Profit minus Cost of Operations)

Max explains how to analyze these numbers for continuous improvement:

1. *Divide the line item value by the Sales value (also known as a **ratio**).*

    Example:

    Materials value $936,491 ÷ Sales value $3,787,179 = .24728.

2. *Move the decimal two places to the right, round off to one decimal place, and change the sign to a percent so that **.24728** becomes **24.7**%*
    Repeat for each line item.

    Example:

    Labor value 644,226 ÷ 3,787,179 = .17011 = 17.0%

Max says to "apply this ratio to every line item and your vertical analysis is done.:

These percentages will become very important, so hang in there with me:

*   *You can now see the total cash received in this period, referred to as **Sales** or **Top Line**, in both dollars and percentages and how much you've spent to operate your business.*

*   *Subtracting all expenses from sales leaves the balance, called **Net Profit** or **Bottom Line**.*

Max's example has what he calls "an important piece of information. You've spent more money than you took in."

If you were to compare income statements for the past two years, scrutinizing the percentages, you'd probably see that the percentages aren't the same. Usually they're not.

Notice the **Net Profit** line. Both totals show a negative 2.2% profit, but the dollar amounts are different. That's because the **Sales** line values are different each year. Since the vertical analysis is a percent of Sales, the dollars always equate the percentage of sales for that year. Now let's compare only the percentages in **Figure 3**. What do we see?

Trust me; this is going to get real interesting in a moment. Overall, we see that even though our sales were different for the two years, we also took a loss both years. We also see that our costs varied by percentage each year. The percentages of costs in each line item were <u>not</u> the same. This tells us something very significant about the organization itself. It appears that top or middle management have lost sight of their financial responsibilities. Perhaps they're not certain what their responsibilities are. We'll look into this more deeply shortly.

For now, let's take each line item at a time. Start with **Materials**. The company spent a greater percentage of its income (**Sales**) on materials in 2008 (24.7%) than it did in 2007 (23.2%). You will notice these small changes in percentages throughout the line items.

What do you suppose would happen if we created another column with the best percentages of the two years? We'll call this third column the <u>Optimal Column</u>. We could then calculate what our cost should have been for the current year of 2008 based on the better percentage performances of the two years.

Here's an example using the materials line item:

In 2008, sales were $3,787,179. We spent 24.7% of that, or $936,491, for materials. But in 2007, we spent only 23.2% for materials. If we'd spent 23.2%

of the $3,787,179 of this year's sales, or $878,625, we'd have saved $57,866 in 2008. WOW!

A few paragraphs above, I spoke of the manager's responsibilities. Who was responsible for letting the cost of materials escalate from 23.2% to 24.7%? Now you can plainly see the consequences of not paying attention to responsibilities or knowing what they are!

Here's the math:

Sales × best percentage of line item = new best cost.

$3,787,179 × 23.2% (instead of 24.7%) = $878,625

Old cost – New cost = savings

$936,491 - $878,625 = $57,866

I told you this would get interesting. Right now, you're trying to jump ahead to see where you can create more savings. Resist the urge until I show you the shortcut.

This company could have shown real profit in both 2008 and 2007. Instead, they lost almost $151,000. Without a sympathetic bank (and a stupid one, I might add, if they lent them any money) or a huge cash reserve, this company will soon be out of business. Even if they pour money into the company, they won't survive if they don't fix the problems: control their costs and learn their responsibilities.

And here's where most business owners who don't understand their financials make the wrong assumption. They believe, with every fiber of their being, that if only they could increase sales, their troubles would be over. You can now see clearly *that if you sell more but your costs in percentages remain the same, you will lose greater and greater amounts of money because on the **Net Profit** line, your percentage of loss will remain the same.*

Let me repeat that: **if you sell more but your costs in percentages remain the same, you will lose greater and greater amounts of money because on the Net Profit line, your percentage of loss will remain the same.**

Ahhhhhhhhh. Enlightenment.

Now let's build that <u>Optimal Column</u> *and see what happens to the bottom line,* **Net Profit***. The first two columns of the P&L statement will remain the same for both years. The third column will display the better percentage of the two years. The fourth will calculate the best new cost using the better percentage, as we did in the above example. The fifth column will show the original 2008 costs and the sixth column will show the difference, the cash that could have been saved.*

OK. Hang on to your hat.

Figure 4:

Line Item	1 2008 %	2 2007 %	3 Best %	4 Best Dollars	5 2008 $$	6 The difference
Current Sales				3,787,179	3,787,179	
materials	24.7	23.2	23.2	878,626	936,491	57,865
labor	17.0	16.4	16.4	621,097	644,226	23,129
subcontractors	2.7	2.3	2.3	87,105	101,098	13,993
Other direct	27.6	31.5	27.6	1,045,261	1,044,284	-977
Sales Salaries	6.7	6.4	6.4	242,379	252,378	9,999
Advertizing	1.0	1.0	1.0	37,872	36,852	-1,020
distribution	0.6	0.7	0.6	22,723	24,001	1,278
Repairs	0.2	0.2	0.2	7,574	8,456	882
Other indirect	1.7	1.6	1.6	60,595	63,869	3,274
Owners Salary	1.9	1.6	1.6	60,595	70,097	9,502
Admin Wages	7.7	6.4	6.4	242,379	290,084	47,705
Depreciation	0.5	0.5	0.5	18,936	17,799	-1,137
Interest Expense	0.2	0.3	0.2	7,574	5,838	-1,736
Facilities	3.0	3.6	3.0	113,615	114,385	770
Other G&A	6.9	6.6	6.6	249,954	259,502	9,548
Net Profit				90,892	(82,181)	173,073

Note: **Because percentages are intentionally rounded to the nearest single decimal and do not use pennies in these calculations, some of the math isn't perfect. It doesn't need to be, because fixing the problems is also not an exact science and will not happen to the nearest penny anyway. These numbers are known as** *performance indicators* **or** *performance metrics*. **There are many other performance indicators, some of which are discussed later.**

If management had known its responsibilities, this company would have shown more than $90,000 in net profit. Instead, they lost more than $82,000 - a difference of about $170,000. The owner of this company didn't know he was leaving $170,000 on the table because he didn't understand what the *company financials were telling him. Although these calculations are fairly simple, they are very time consuming. CFO-Genie software, found at cfogenie. com or ceo1stop.com, will get you off the hook. A simple click of the mouse will automate this entire calculation for you and do the horizontal analysis for up to four years or four time periods.*

Analyzing three time periods is better than analyzing two, and four is better than three. More than four is usually unnecessary. However, if you want to do some interesting analyses, try using time periods that aren't sequential. But always use the current period in the first column.

And now you have it: where you are, and where you could have been if you'd had the information sooner. OK. Now you have the information. What can you do with it?

You can now create next year's budget. If you use the optimal burn rate in percentages, as shown in **Figure 5**, *and estimate your sales, you can calculate the dollars you need for each line item and see your net profit ahead of time. Remember the formula?*

Sales X Line Item % = best new Cost for that Line Item.

Of course, this means that management must be responsible for toeing the line, so to speak, and keep those costs in check. But now you know what those costs are supposed to be based, at this point, on historical best performance.

Max then moves into an area of leadership responsibility—helping employees understand the difference between their "duty" and their "responsibility."

When I'm hired by a company to determine the root cause of a cost problem, I usually speak to the person responsible for controlling that line item percentage (hopefully, there is such a person, or the company may have bigger problems). Let's assume I'll be speaking with the accounts receivable clerk. This person's **duty** *is to collect receivables. This person's* **responsibility,** *on the other hand, is to make certain no receivables go beyond 30 days (or whatever length of time is customary in that industry).*

*Why is this important? Let's examine what happens to a company that allows receivables go to 40 days instead of making certain the money is received in 30 days. Let's also assume the company's top line (***Net Sales***) is $1,440,000. Divide that by 12 and you have monthly sales of $120,000. Divide $120,000 by 30 and you have daily sales of $4,000. That means that this company always has $120,000 in receivables if the money is collected on time. But for every day that passes after 30, $4,000 is added to the total receivables. At 40 days, there's an extra $40,000, or a total of $160,000, in receivables. If you were the owner of this company, wouldn't you want to have that extra $40,000 in your check book? I'm sure you could find plenty of business-enhancing things to do with that money if it were available ... things that would give you a return on the investment ... or ROI.*

Now don't go and fire your Accounts Receivable person, or anyone else, for that matter. Just make certain they're trained to know their **duties** *and* **responsibilities.**

One of Max's key points in discussing the financial implications of continuous improvement is to understand the concept of "investing in" rather than "spending on" in calculating expenses.

Every time your company pays for something, you're investing in that item, not spending for it. This enables a new frame of mind that tells you that you must always get a return on your investment. Most small business owners see expenses as "the cost of doing business." If it truly is the cost of doing business, your mind automatically equates that with a loss. This is <u>absolutely</u> *the* <u>wrong frame of mind</u>.

Think about this for a moment: Would you invest your hard-earned money in anything, and I mean anything, that promised either no return or an actual loss? Hmmm. Could this be more enlightenment? I'll say it is. I can't tell you how many times I've heard the phrase, "It's the cost of doing business." It's a phrase people use when they know they're spending hard-earned cash on something that will return nothing. I said it myself in my early career as a business owner. I've learned that this frame of mind cost me dearly. But just a slight shift in perspective can change everything. <u>Invest</u> *instead of* <u>spend</u>*!*

Here's an example of that mistake: Company owner Bob spends money on advertising. The phone never rings. Bob has never attracted a new customer from his advertising. Bob believes that he must present the company in advertisements or his customers will think he's gone out of business. He says, "It's the cost of doing business." There's that phrase again. Can you see what's wrong with this picture? In a general sense, it's easy to see that there is something wrong. But how do you quantify it so you can really understand the consequences of "the phrase"?

Let's do some ratios. Bob has sales of $1,000,000 and spends $50,000 on advertising. At first glance, it appears that 5% of his income (sales) is spent on advertising. In reality, this ratio is not that bad. The ratio is actually a true statement -- except that if advertising doesn't get the phone to ring and Bob never gets any new customers from this advertising, he needs to see the problem from a different perspective. Bob says that if he doesn't advertise, his customers will think he's gone out of business. What would it cost Bob to do a direct mailing to his current customers just to let them know he's still around? Perhaps it would be somewhat less than $50,000. It might only cost him $5,000. Now his ratio is 0.5%, which is much better than 5% and it solves the problem of letting his current customers know he's still in business. But Bob would still like to advertise to try to get new customers. How can he monitor his ROI? Suppose he separates his sales into two categories: Current Customer Sales (CCS) and New Customer Sales (NCS). Then he can calculate ratios on percentage ROI for each category separately.

Example: Bob has a total of $50,000 to invest in advertising.

CCS = $1,000,000: Direct mail = $5,000

ROI = 20,000%

NCS = $0,   Advertising $45,000 = $0

ROI = 0% ????

Bob now gets 20,000% ROI for his direct mail piece but zero ROI for his advertising. Bob should certainly stop his advertising campaign quickly and would have to develop a new marketing strategy for NCS that would definitely give him a ROI.

The lesson here is that thinking "investment" instead of "spending" changes your perspective -- and your *profitability. Bob has just added $45,000 to his Net Profit by eliminating an advertising investment that doesn't work because there is no ROI.*

But what if Bob found a new marketing strategy? Let's say he found that by advertising in a trade magazine instead of the newspaper his phone began to ring, and every time he ran the ad, he got on average one new customer worth $40,000 in sales.

The ad cost him $2,000 and could be placed once a month. In 12 months, it would cost $12,000 but he would receive 12 new customers worth a total of $480,000. Let's look at the ratios now.

CCS = $1,000,000: Direct mail = $ 5,000

ROI = 20,000%

NCS = $480,000: Advertising = $12,000

ROI = 4,000%

Eureka!

Since it usually costs five times more to create a new customer than to keep an old one, this ratio works perfectly and is an apparent success. But you still need to examine the profitability from new customers before you declare complete success. Can this ROI still be improved? Most likely it can.

Income Statement (see fig. 2)		Calculated Ratio	Formula
Sales	$ 3,787,179		
Expense:			
Materials	$ 936,491	4.04	Sales ÷ the expense
Labor	$ 644,226	5.88	Sales ÷ the expense
Subcontractors	$ 101,098	37.46	Sales ÷ the expense
Sales Salaries	$ 252,378	15.01	Sales ÷ the expense
Advertizing	$ 36,852	102.77	Sales ÷ the expense
Admin Wages	$ 290,084	13.06	Sales ÷ the expense
Facilities Expenses	$ 114,385	33.11	Sales ÷ the expense

Figure 6

When comparing **expenses** *with* **sales** *- the higher the ratio the better. By the way, since this example is calculated in dollars,* **Figure 6** *also shows the return on investment for each line item ... i.e. for every dollar invested in material you receive $4.04 return. To get the percentage just move the decimal two places to the right and you'll see the return of 404% for materials.*

And that's some of what Max Gregorich has to say about the numbers in kaizen/continuous improvement. There's much more, all of it available on Max's web site, www.ceo1stop.com.

NOTES

Chapter 12

"Cash Machine" Yes or No: The Choice Is Yours

Getting your organization started on becoming a kaizen/ continuous improvement Cash Machine generates an interesting, if somewhat abbreviated decision tree. Let's take a look:

Kaizen/continuous improvement, yes or no?

- If no, continue doing things the way you always did them, in which case you can stop reading at this point.

- If yes, create a plan to jump start your kaizen transition.

Use ISO to jump start your kaizen/continuous improvement transition, yes or no?

- If no, try some other means to get into the kaizen game. There are plenty of approaches out there; one of them may be right for you.

- If yes, consider finding an ISO consultant to help you prepare for your audit. We can help. Contact Greg at gab4iso.com for a list of qualified ISO consultants in your area.

Once these decisions have been made, the rest of your relationship with kaizen/continuous improvement can be determined along the way. Your ISO certification will give you vital information on your readiness for kaizen.

We predict that you'll have a pleasant surprise when you learn that you have more kaizen capabilities than you anticipated. For example, you'll likely have employees who are eager to participate in improving their work processes, once they understand what's in it for them in a kaizen organization.

You can use your ISO results as the raw materials for developing your training and communication plans. You can use Max Gregorich's financial anaysis systems to identify areas where continuous improvement can provide the most Cash Machine gains.

You can use our earlier approaches for forming and managing problem-solving teams, making modifications along the way that meet your unique needs. Check www.gab4iso.com for updated ideas about what has worked at our client organizations.

The rest is up to you. Contact us with your questions, suggestions, and experiences with your Cash Machine.

And stay away from masked men riding white horses.

NOTES

NOTES